ⳤⵕⴹⴶⵎⵏⵉⴹⳤ
Translated Language Learning

The Communist Manifesto
共产党宣言

Karl Marx & Friedrich Engels

English / 普通话

Published by Tranzlaty
ISBN: 978-1-83566-229-8
Original text by Karl Marx and Friedrich Engels
The Communist Manifesto
First published in 1848
www.tranzlaty.com

Introduction
介绍

A spectre is haunting Europe — the spectre of Communism
一个幽灵正在困扰着欧洲——共产主义的幽灵

All the Powers of old Europe have entered into a holy alliance to exorcise this spectre
旧欧洲的所有大国都结成了神圣的联盟，以驱除这个幽灵

Pope and Czar, Metternich and Guizot, French Radicals and German police-spies
教皇和沙皇，梅特涅和吉佐，法国激进分子和德国警察间谍

Where is the party in opposition that has not been decried as Communistic by its opponents in power?
没有被执政对手谴责为共产主义的反对党在哪里？

Where is the Opposition that has not hurled back the branding reproach of Communism, against the more advanced opposition parties?
没有反击共产主义的烙印指责，反对更先进的反对党的反对派在哪里？

And where is the party that has not made the accusation against its reactionary adversaries?
没有对其反动对手提出指控的政党在哪里？

Two things result from this fact
这一事实导致了两件事

I. Communism is already acknowledged by all European Powers to be itself a Power
一、所有欧洲列强都承认共产主义本身就是一个大国

II. It is high time that Communists should openly, in the face of the whole world, publish their views, aims and tendencies
二、现在是共产党人当着全世界的面公开发表自己的观点、宗旨和倾向的时候了

they must meet this nursery tale of the Spectre of Communism with a Manifesto of the party itself
他们必须用党本身的宣言来迎接这个共产主义幽灵的童话故事

To this end, Communists of various nationalities have assembled in London and sketched the following Manifesto

为此，各民族的共产党人聚集在伦敦，草拟了以下宣言

this manifesto is to be published in the English, French, German, Italian, Flemish and Danish languages

该宣言将以英文、法文、德文、意大利文、佛兰芒文和丹麦文出版

And now it is to be published in all the languages that Tranzlaty offers

现在，它将以 Tranzlaty 提供的所有语言出版

Bourgeois and the Proletarians
资产阶级和无产者

The history of all hitherto existing societies is the history of class struggles

迄今为止所有现存社会的历史都是阶级斗争的历史

Freeman and slave, patrician and plebeian, lord and serf, guild-master and journeyman

自由人与奴隶，贵族与平民，领主与农奴，行会主与工匠

in a word, oppressor and oppressed

一句话，压迫者和被压迫者

these social classes stood in constant opposition to one another

这些社会阶层不断相互对立

they carried on an uninterrupted fight. Now hidden, now open

他们进行了不间断的战斗。现在隐藏，现在打开

a fight that either ended in a revolutionary re-constitution of society at large

这场斗争要么以整个社会的革命性重建而告终

or a fight that ended in the common ruin of the contending classes

或者是一场以相互竞争的阶级共同毁灭而告终的斗争

let us look back to the earlier epochs of history

让我们回顾一下历史的早期时代

we find almost everywhere a complicated arrangement of society into various orders

我们几乎到处都发现社会的复杂安排，分为各种秩序

there has always been a manifold gradation of social rank

社会等级一直存在多种等级

In ancient Rome we have patricians, knights, plebeians, slaves

在古罗马，我们有贵族、骑士、平民、奴隶

in the Middle Ages: feudal lords, vassals, guild-masters, journeymen, apprentices, serfs

中世纪：封建领主、附庸、行会大师、工匠、学徒、农奴

in almost all of these classes, again, subordinate gradations

在几乎所有这些类别中，同样是从属等级

The modern Bourgeoisie society has sprouted from the ruins of feudal society

现代资产阶级社会是从封建社会的废墟中萌芽出来的

but this new social order has not done away with class antagonisms

但这种新的社会秩序并没有消除阶级对立

It has but established new classes and new conditions of oppression

它只是建立了新的阶级和新的压迫条件

it has established new forms of struggle in place of the old ones

它建立了新的斗争形式来取代旧的斗争形式

however, the epoch we find ourselves in possesses one distinctive feature

然而，我们所处的时代具有一个鲜明的特征

the epoch of the Bourgeoisie has simplified the class antagonisms

资产阶级时代简化了阶级对立

Society as a whole is more and more splitting up into two great hostile camps

整个社会越来越分裂成两大敌对阵营

two great social classes directly facing each other: Bourgeoisie and Proletariat

两个直接对立的大社会阶级：资产阶级和无产阶级

From the serfs of the Middle Ages sprang the chartered burghers of the earliest towns

从中世纪的农奴中涌现出最早城镇的特许市民

From these burgesses the first elements of the Bourgeoisie were developed

从这些市民那里发展了资产阶级的第一批元素

The discovery of America and the rounding of the Cape

美洲的发现和开普敦的四舍五入

these events opened up fresh ground for the rising Bourgeoisie

这些事件为崛起的资产阶级开辟了新天地

The East-Indian and Chinese markets, the colonisation of

America, trade with the colonies
东印度和中国市场，美洲的殖民化，与殖民地的贸易
the increase in the means of exchange and in commodities generally
交换资料和一般商品的增加
these events gave to commerce, navigation, and industry an impulse never before known
这些事件给商业、航海和工业带来了前所未有的推动力
it gave rapid development to the revolutionary element in the tottering feudal society
它使摇摇欲坠的封建社会的革命因素迅速发展
closed guilds had monopolised the feudal system of industrial production
封闭的行会垄断了封建的工业生产体系
but this no longer sufficed for the growing wants of the new markets
但这已经不足以满足新市场日益增长的需求
The manufacturing system took the place of the feudal system of industry
制造体系取代了封建工业体系
The guild-masters were pushed on one side by the manufacturing middle class
行会会长被制造业中产阶级推到一边
division of labour between the different corporate guilds vanished
不同公司行会之间的分工消失了
the division of labour penetrated each single workshop
劳动分工渗透到每个车间
Meantime, the markets kept ever growing, and the demand ever rising
与此同时，市场不断增长，需求不断上升
Even factories no longer sufficed to meet the demands
即使是工厂也不再足以满足需求
Thereupon, steam and machinery revolutionised industrial production
因此，蒸汽和机械彻底改变了工业生产
The place of manufacture was taken by the giant, Modern

Industry

制造地点被巨大的现代工业所取代

the place of the industrial middle class was taken by
industrial millionaires

工业中产阶级的位置被工业百万富翁取代

the place of leaders of whole industrial armies were taken
by the modern Bourgeoisie

整个工业军队的领导人的位置被现代资产阶级所取代

the discovery of America paved the way for modern industry
to establish the world market

美洲的发现为现代工业建立世界市场铺平了道路

This market gave an immense development to commerce,
navigation, and communication by land

这个市场为陆路商业、航海和通信带来了巨大的发展

This development has, in its time, reacted on the extension
of industry

在当时，这种发展对工业的扩展做出了反应

it reacted in proportion to how industry extended, and how
commerce, navigation and railways extended

它的反应与工业如何扩展以及商业、航海和铁路如何扩展成正
比

in the same proportion that the Bourgeoisie developed, they
increased their capital

按照资产阶级发展的比例，他们增加了资本

and the Bourgeoisie pushed into the background every class
handed down from the Middle Ages

资产阶级将中世纪流传下来的每一个阶级都推到了幕后

therefore the modern Bourgeoisie is itself the product of a
long course of development

因此，现代资产阶级本身就是长期发展过程的产物

we see it is a series of revolutions in the modes of
production and of exchange

我们看到，这是生产方式和交换方式的一系列革命

Each developmental Bourgeoisie step was accompanied by a
corresponding political advance

资产阶级的每一步发展都伴随着相应的政治进步

An oppressed class under the sway of the feudal nobility

封建贵族统治下的被压迫阶级

an armed and self-governing association in the mediaeval commune

中世纪公社的武装自治协会

here, an independent urban republic (as in Italy and Germany)

在这里，一个独立的城市共和国（如意大利和德国）

there, a taxable "third estate" of the monarchy (as in France)

在那里，君主制的应税"第三等级"（如法国）

afterwards, in the period of manufacture proper

之后，在适当的制造期间

the Bourgeoisie served either the semi-feudal or the absolute monarchy

资产阶级要么服务于半封建君主制，要么服务于绝对君主制

or the Bourgeoisie acted as a counterpoise against the nobility

或者资产阶级充当了对贵族的反击

and, in fact, the Bourgeoisie was a corner-stone of the great monarchies in general

事实上，资产阶级是大君主制的基石

but Modern Industry and the world-market established itself since then

但从那时起，现代工业和世界市场就确立了自己的地位

and the Bourgeoisie has conquered for itself exclusive political sway

资产阶级已经为自己赢得了排他性的政治影响力

it achieved this political sway through the modern representative State

它通过现代代议制国家实现了这种政治影响力

The executives of the modern State are but a management committee

现代国家的行政人员只不过是一个管理委员会

and they manage the common affairs of the whole of the Bourgeoisie

他们管理整个资产阶级的共同事务

The Bourgeoisie, historically, has played a most revolutionary part

从历史上看，资产阶级发挥了最具革命性的作用

wherever it got the upper hand, it put an end to all feudal, patriarchal, and idyllic relations

无论它在哪里占上风，它都结束了所有封建、父权制和田园诗般的关系

It has pitilessly torn asunder the motley feudal ties that bound man to his "natural superiors"

它无情地撕毁了将人束缚在"天生的上级"身上的杂乱无章的封建关系

and it has left remaining no nexus between man and man, other than naked self-interest

除了赤裸裸的利己主义之外，人与人之间没有任何联系

man's relations with one another have become nothing more than callous "cash payment"

人与人之间的关系只不过是冷酷无情的"现金支付"

It has drowned the most heavenly ecstasies of religious fervour

它淹没了宗教狂热的最天堂般的狂喜

it has drowned chivalrous enthusiasm and philistine sentimentalism

它淹没了骑士的热情和庸俗的感伤主义

it has drowned these things in the icy water of egotistical calculation

它把这些东西淹没在自负的计算的冰水中

It has resolved personal worth into exchangeable value

它把个人价值化为可交换的价值

it has replaced the numberless and indefeasible chartered freedoms

它取代了无数和不可剥夺的宪章自由

and it has set up a single, unconscionable freedom; Free Trade

它建立了一个单一的、不合情理的自由;自由贸易

In one word, it has done this for exploitation

一言以蔽之，它这样做是为了剥削

exploitation veiled by religious and political illusions

被宗教和政治幻想所掩盖的剥削

exploitation veiled by naked, shameless, direct, brutal

exploitation
赤裸裸的、无耻的、直接的、残酷的剥削所掩盖的剥削

the Bourgeoisie has stripped the halo off every previously honoured and revered occupation
资产阶级已经剥夺了以前所有受人尊敬和尊敬的职业的光环

the physician, the lawyer, the priest, the poet, and the man of science
医生、律师、牧师、诗人和科学家

it has converted these distinguished workers into its paid wage labourers
它把这些杰出的工人变成了有偿的雇佣劳动者

The Bourgeoisie has torn the sentimental veil away from the family
资产阶级已经撕下了家庭的感伤面纱

and it has reduced the family relation to a mere money relation
它把家庭关系简化为单纯的金钱关系

the brutal display of vigour in the Middle Ages which Reactionists so much admire
反动派非常钦佩的中世纪残酷的活力表现

even this found its fitting complement in the most slothful indolence
即使这样，在最懒惰的懒惰中也找到了合适的补充

The Bourgeoisie has disclosed how all this came to pass
资产阶级已经揭露了这一切是如何发生的

The Bourgeoisie have been the first to show what man's activity can bring about
资产阶级是第一个表明人的活动可以带来什么的人

It has accomplished wonders far surpassing Egyptian pyramids, Roman aqueducts, and Gothic cathedrals
它所创造的奇迹远远超过了埃及金字塔、罗马渡槽和哥特式大教堂

and it has conducted expeditions that put in the shade all former Exoduses of nations and crusades
它进行了远征，使所有以前的国家流亡和十字军东征都蒙上了阴影

The Bourgeoisie cannot exist without constantly

revolutionising the instruments of production
如果不不断革新生产工具，资产阶级就不可能存在
and thereby it cannot exist without its relations to production
因此，没有它与生产的关系，它就不能存在
and therefore it cannot exist without its relations to society
因此，没有它与社会的关系，它就不可能存在
all earlier industrial classes had one condition in common
所有早期的工业阶级都有一个共同点
they relied on the conservation of the old modes of production
他们依靠对旧生产方式的保护
but the Bourgeoisie brought with it a completely new dynamic
但资产阶级带来了一种全新的动力
Constant revolutionizing of production and uninterrupted disturbance of all social conditions
生产的不断革命和一切社会条件的不间断的干扰
this everlasting uncertainty and agitation distinguishes the Bourgeoisie epoch from all earlier ones
这种永恒的不确定性和躁动性使资产阶级时代有别于所有早期的时代
previous relations with production came with ancient and venerable prejudices and opinions
以前与生产的关系伴随着古老而古老的偏见和观点
but all of these fixed, fast-frozen relations are swept away
但所有这些固定的、快速冻结的关系都被一扫而空
all new-formed relations become antiquated before they can ossify
所有新形成的关系在僵化之前就已经过时了
All that is solid melts into air, and all that is holy is profaned
所有固体都融化成空气，所有神圣的东西都被亵渎了
man is at last compelled to face with sober senses, his real conditions of life
人终于不得不以清醒的感官面对他的真实生活状况
and he is compelled to face his relations with his kind
他被迫面对他与同类的关系

The Bourgeoisie constantly needs to expand its markets for
its products
资产阶级不断需要扩大其产品的市场

and, because of this, the Bourgeoisie is chased over the
whole surface of the globe
正因为如此，资产阶级在整个地球表面都被追逐

The Bourgeoisie must nestle everywhere, settle everywhere,
establish connections everywhere
资产阶级必须到处依偎，到处定居，到处建立联系

The Bourgeoisie must create markets in every corner of the
world to exploit
资产阶级必须在世界每个角落创造市场来剥削

the production and consumption in every country has been
given a cosmopolitan character
每个国家的生产和消费都被赋予了世界性的特征

the chagrin of Reactionists is palpable, but it has carried on
regardless
反动派的懊恼是显而易见的，但无论如何它仍在继续

The Bourgeoisie have drawn from under the feet of industry
the national ground on which it stood
资产阶级从工业的脚下汲取了它赖以生存的民族土地

all old-established national industries have been destroyed,
or are daily being destroyed
所有老牌的民族工业都已被摧毁，或每天都在被摧毁

all old-established national industries are dislodged by new
industries
所有老牌的民族工业都被新工业所取代

their introduction becomes a life and death question for all
civilised nations
它们的引入成为所有文明国家的生死攸关的问题

they are dislodged by industries that no longer work up
indigenous raw material
他们被不再使用本土原材料的工业所取代

instead, these industries pull raw materials from the
remotest zones
相反，这些行业从最偏远的地区提取原材料

industries whose products are consumed, not only at home,

but in every quarter of the globe

其产品不仅在国内，而且在全球每个季度都被消费的行业

In place of the old wants, satisfied by the productions of the country, we find new wants

代替旧的需求，通过国家的产品来满足，我们找到了新的需求

these new wants require for their satisfaction the products of distant lands and climes

这些新的需求需要来自遥远的土地和气候的产品来满足它们

In place of the old local and national seclusion and self-sufficiency, we have trade

取而代之的是旧的地方和国家隔离和自给自足，我们有贸易

international exchange in every direction; universal inter-dependence of nations

四面八方的国际交流;各国普遍相互依存

and just as we have dependency on materials, so we are dependent on intellectual production

正如我们依赖材料一样，我们也依赖于智力生产

The intellectual creations of individual nations become common property

各个民族的智力创造成为共同财产

National one-sidedness and narrow-mindedness become more and more impossible

民族的片面性和狭隘性越来越不可能

and from the numerous national and local literatures, there arises a world literature

从众多的国家和地方文学中，产生了世界文学

by the rapid improvement of all instruments of production

通过所有生产工具的快速改进

by the immensely facilitated means of communication

通过极其便利的沟通方式

The Bourgeoisie draws all (even the most barbarian nations) into civilisation

资产阶级把所有国家（甚至是最野蛮的民族）都吸引到文明中来

The cheap prices of its commodities; the heavy artillery that batters down all Chinese walls

其商品的廉价价格;重炮摧毁了所有中国城墙

the barbarians' intensely obstinate hatred of foreigners is forced to capitulate

野蛮人对外国人的强烈顽固仇恨被迫投降

It compels all nations, on pain of extinction, to adopt the Bourgeoisie mode of production

它迫使所有民族在濒临灭绝的痛苦中采用资产阶级的生产方式

it compels them to introduce what it calls civilisation into their midst

它迫使他们把所谓的文明引入他们中间

The Bourgeoisie force the barbarians to become Bourgeoisie themselves

资产阶级强迫野蛮人自己成为资产阶级

in a word, the Bourgeoisie creates a world after its own image

一句话，资产阶级按照自己的形象创造了一个世界

The Bourgeoisie has subjected the countryside to the rule of the towns

资产阶级把农村置于城镇的统治之下

It has created enormous cities and greatly increased the urban population

它创造了巨大的城市，大大增加了城市人口

it rescued a considerable part of the population from the idiocy of rural life

它把相当一部分人口从农村生活的愚蠢中解救出来

but it has made those in the the countryside dependent on the towns

但它使农村的人依赖城镇

and likewise, it has made the barbarian countries dependent on the civilised ones

同样，它使野蛮国家依赖文明国家

nations of peasants on nations of Bourgeoisie, the East on the West

农民国家对资产阶级国家，东方对西方国家

The Bourgeoisie does away with the scattered state of the population more and more

资产阶级越来越消除人口的分散状态

It has agglomerated production, and has concentrated

property in a few hands
它集中了生产，并将财产集中在少数人手中
The necessary consequence of this was political centralisation
其必然后果是政治集权
there had been independent nations and loosely connected provinces
曾经有过独立的国家和松散联系的省份
they had separate interests, laws, governments and systems of taxation
他们有各自的利益、法律、政府和税收制度
but they have become lumped together into one nation, with one government
但是他们已经混为一谈，组成一个国家，一个政府
they now have one national class-interest, one frontier and one customs-tariff
他们现在有一个国家阶级利益，一个边界和一个关税
and this national class-interest is unified under one code of law
这种民族阶级利益统一在一个法典之下
the Bourgeoisie has achieved much during its rule of scarce one hundred years
资产阶级在其短短的一百年统治中取得了很大的成就
more massive and colossal productive forces than have all preceding generations together
比前几代人加起来还要庞大和巨大的生产力
Nature's forces are subjugated to the will of man and his machinery
自然的力量屈服于人的意志及其机器
chemistry is applied to all forms of industry and types of agriculture
化学应用于所有形式的工业和农业类型
steam-navigation, railways, electric telegraphs, and the printing press
蒸汽航海、铁路、电报和印刷机
clearing of whole continents for cultivation, canalisation of rivers

清理整个大陆进行耕种，河流渠化

whole populations have been conjured out of the ground and put to work

整个人口都被从地下召唤出来并投入工作

what earlier century had even a presentiment of what could be unleashed?

哪个上个世纪甚至预感到可以释放什么？

who predicted that such productive forces slumbered in the lap of social labour?

谁能预料到这样的生产力会沉睡在社会劳动的怀抱中？

we see then that the means of production and of exchange were generated in feudal society

我们看到，生产资料和交换资料是在封建社会中产生的

the means of production on whose foundation the Bourgeoisie built itself up

资产阶级赖以建立自己的生产资料

At a certain stage in the development of these means of production and of exchange

在这些生产资料和交换资料发展的某个阶段

the conditions under which feudal society produced and exchanged

封建社会生产和交换的条件

the feudal organisation of agriculture and manufacturing industry

农业和制造业的封建组织

the feudal relations of property were no longer compatible with the material conditions

封建财产关系不再与物质条件相容

They had to be burst asunder, so they were burst asunder

他们必须被爆裂，所以他们被爆裂了

Into their place stepped free competition from the productive forces

取而代之的是生产力的自由竞争

and they were accompanied by a social and political constitution adapted to it

他们伴随着与之相适应的社会和政治宪法

and it was accompanied by the economical and political

sway of the Bourgeoisie class
它伴随着资产阶级的经济和政治影响力

A similar movement is going on before our own eyes
类似的运动正在我们眼前发生

Modern Bourgeoisie society with its relations of production, and of exchange, and of property
现代资产阶级社会及其生产关系、交换关系和财产关系

a society that has conjured up such gigantic means of production and of exchange
一个创造了如此巨大的生产资料和交换资料的社会

it is like the sorcerer who called up the powers of the nether world
这就像召唤下界力量的巫师

but he is no longer able to control what he has brought into the world
但他再也无法控制他带给世界的东西

For many a decade past history was tied together by a common thread
在过去的十年里，历史被一条共同的线索联系在一起

the history of industry and commerce has been but the history of revolts
工商业的历史不过是起义的历史

the revolts of modern productive forces against modern conditions of production
现代生产力对现代生产条件的反抗

the revolts of modern productive forces against property relations
现代生产力对财产关系的反抗

these property relations are the conditions for the existence of the Bourgeoisie
这些财产关系是资产阶级存在的条件

and the existence of the Bourgeoisie determines the rules for property relations
资产阶级的存在决定了财产关系的规则

it is enough to mention the periodical return of commercial crises
提到商业危机的周期性回归就足够了

each commercial crisis is more threatening to Bourgeoisie society than the last

每一次商业危机对资产阶级社会的威胁都比上一次更大

In these crises a great part of the existing products are destroyed

在这些危机中，现有产品的很大一部分被摧毁

but these crises also destroy the previously created productive forces

但这些危机也摧毁了先前创造的生产力

in all earlier epochs these epidemics would have seemed an absurdity

在所有更早的时代，这些流行病似乎是荒谬的

because these epidemics are the commercial crises of over-production

因为这些流行病是生产过剩的商业危机

Society suddenly finds itself put back into a state of momentary barbarism

社会突然发现自己又回到了短暂的野蛮状态

as if a universal war of devastation had cut off every means of subsistence

仿佛一场普遍的毁灭性战争切断了一切生存手段

industry and commerce seem to have been destroyed; and why?

工商业似乎被摧毁了;为什么？

Because there is too much civilisation and means of subsistence

因为有太多的文明和生存手段

and because there is too much industry, and too much commerce

因为有太多的工业和太多的商业

The productive forces at the disposal of society no longer develop Bourgeoisie property

社会所支配的生产力不再发展资产阶级财产

on the contrary, they have become too powerful for these conditions, by which they are fettered

相反，对于这些条件来说，他们已经变得太强大了，他们被束缚了

as soon as they overcome these fetters, they bring disorder
into the whole of Bourgeoisie society
一旦他们克服了这些束缚，他们就会给整个资产阶级社会带来
混乱

and the productive forces endanger the existence of
Bourgeoisie property
生产力危及资产阶级财产的生存

The conditions of Bourgeoisie society are too narrow to
comprise the wealth created by them
资产阶级社会的条件太狭隘，无法包括他们创造的财富

And how does the Bourgeoisie get over these crises?
资产阶级如何克服这些危机？

On the one hand, it overcomes these crises by the enforced
destruction of a mass of productive forces
一方面，它通过强行摧毁大量生产力来克服这些危机

on the other hand, it overcomes these crises by the conquest
of new markets
另一方面，它通过征服新市场来克服这些危机

and it overcomes these crises by the more thorough
exploitation of the old forces of production
它通过更彻底地剥削旧的生产力量来克服这些危机

That is to say, by paving the way for more extensive and
more destructive crises
也就是说，为更广泛和更具破坏性的危机铺平道路

it overcomes the crisis by diminishing the means whereby
crises are prevented
它通过减少预防危机的手段来克服危机

The weapons with which the Bourgeoisie felled feudalism
to the ground are now turned against itself
资产阶级用来把封建主义打倒在地的武器现在正对着自己

But not only has the Bourgeoisie forged the weapons that
bring death to itself
但是，资产阶级不仅锻造了给自己带来死亡的武器

it has also called into existence the men who are to wield
those weapons
它还召唤了将要使用这些武器的人

and these men are the modern working class; they are the

proletarians
这些人是现代工人阶级;他们是无产者

In proportion as the Bourgeoisie is developed, in the same proportion is the Proletariat developed
资产阶级的发展与资产阶级的发展成比例相同

the modern working class developed a class of labourers
现代工人阶级发展出一个劳动者阶级

this class of labourers live only so long as they find work
这一类劳动者只要找到工作，就只能活下去

and they find work only so long as their labour increases capital
他们只有在劳动增加资本的情况下才能找到工作

These labourers, who must sell themselves piece-meal, are a commodity
这些必须零敲碎打地出卖自己的劳动者是一种商品

these labourers are like every other article of commerce
这些劳动者就像其他所有商业物品一样

and they are consequently exposed to all the vicissitudes of competition
因此，他们暴露在竞争的所有沧桑之中

they have to weather all the fluctuations of the market
他们必须经受住市场的所有波动

Owing to the extensive use of machinery and to division of labour
由于机器的广泛使用和劳动分工

the work of the proletarians has lost all individual character
无产者的工作已经丧失了一切个人特征

and consequently, the work of the proletarians has lost all charm for the workman
因此，无产者的工作对工人失去了一切魅力

He becomes an appendage of the machine, rather than the man he once was
他变成了机器的附属物，而不是他曾经的人

only the most simple, monotonous, and most easily acquired knack is required of him
他只需要最简单、最单调、最容易获得的诀窍

Hence, the cost of production of a workman is restricted

因此，工人的生产成本受到限制

it is restricted almost entirely to the means of subsistence that he requires for his maintenance

它几乎完全限于他维持生活所需的生活资料

and it is restricted to the means of subsistence that he requires for the propagation of his race

它仅限于他繁衍种族所需的生活资料

But the price of a commodity, and therefore also of labour, is equal to its cost of production

但是，商品的价格，因此也包括劳动力的价格，等于它的生产成本

In proportion, therefore, as the repulsiveness of the work increases, the wage decreases

因此，随着工作的排斥性增加，工资就会按比例下降

Nay, the repulsiveness of his work increases at an even greater rate

不，他工作的令人厌恶的速度甚至更大

as the use of machinery and division of labour increases, so does the burden of toil

随着机器的使用和劳动分工的增加，劳动的负担也在增加

the burden of toil is increased by prolongation of the working hours

劳动时间的延长增加了辛劳的负担

more is expected of the labourer in the same time as before

与以前一样，对劳动者的期望更高

and of course the burden of the toil is increased by the speed of the machinery

当然，机器的速度会增加辛劳的负担

Modern industry has converted the little workshop of the patriarchal master into the great factory of the industrial capitalist

现代工业已经把父权制主人的小作坊变成了工业资本家的大工厂

Masses of labourers, crowded into the factory, are organised like soldiers

大批工人挤进工厂，像士兵一样组织起来

As privates of the industrial army they are placed under the command of a perfect hierarchy of officers and sergeants

作为工业军队的士兵，他们被置于完美的军官和中士等级制度的指挥之下

they are not only the slaves of the Bourgeoisie class and State

他们不仅是资产阶级和国家的奴隶

but they are also daily and hourly enslaved by the machine

但他们也每天和每小时都受到机器的奴役

they are enslaved by the over-looker, and, above all, by the individual Bourgeoisie manufacturer himself

他们被监督者所奴役，尤其是被个别资产阶级制造商自己所奴役

The more openly this despotism proclaims gain to be its end and aim, the more petty, the more hateful and the more embittering it is

这种专制主义越是公开宣称利益是它的目的和目标，它就越是卑鄙、越可恨、越令人痛苦

the more modern industry becomes developed, the lesser are the differences between the sexes

现代工业越发达，两性之间的差异就越小

The less the skill and exertion of strength implied in manual labour, the more is the labour of men superseded by that of women

体力劳动所隐含的技能和力量消耗越少，男性的劳动就越多被妇女的劳动所取代

Differences of age and sex no longer have any distinctive social validity for the working class

对于工人阶级来说，年龄和性别的差异不再具有任何独特的社会有效性

All are instruments of labour, more or less expensive to use, according to their age and sex

所有这些都是劳动工具，根据他们的年龄和性别，使用起来或多或少是昂贵的

as soon as the labourer receives his wages in cash, than he is set upon by the other portions of the Bourgeoisie

工人一拿到现金工资，资产阶级的其他部分就对他不利

the landlord, the shopkeeper, the pawnbroker, etc

房东、店主、典当行等
The lower strata of the middle class; the small trades people and shopkeepers
中产阶级的下层;小商人和店主
the retired tradesmen generally, and the handicraftsmen and peasants
一般是退休的商人，手工业者和农民
all these sink gradually into the Proletariat
所有这些都逐渐沉入无产阶级
partly because their diminutive capital does not suffice for the scale on which Modern Industry is carried on
部分原因是他们微薄的资本不足以维持现代工业的规模
and because it is swamped in the competition with the large capitalists
因为它在与大资本家的竞争中被淹没了
partly because their specialized skill is rendered worthless by the new methods of production
部分原因是他们的专业技能因新的生产方法而变得毫无价值
Thus the Proletariat is recruited from all classes of the population
因此，无产阶级是从各阶层人口中招募的
The Proletariat goes through various stages of development
无产阶级经历了不同的发展阶段
With its birth begins its struggle with the Bourgeoisie
随着它的诞生，它开始了与资产阶级的斗争
At first the contest is carried on by individual labourers
起初，比赛是由个体劳动者进行的
then the contest is carried on by the workpeople of a factory
然后比赛由工厂的工人进行
then the contest is carried on by the operatives of one trade, in one locality
然后比赛由一个地方的一个行业的操作人员进行
and the contest is then against the individual Bourgeoisie who directly exploits them
然后，竞争是针对直接剥削他们的个别资产阶级的
They direct their attacks not against the Bourgeoisie conditions of production

他们攻击的不是资产阶级的生产条件

but they direct their attack against the instruments of production themselves

但是他们把攻击指向生产工具本身

they destroy imported wares that compete with their labour

他们销毁与他们的劳动力竞争的进口商品

they smash to pieces machinery and they set factories ablaze

他们把机器砸得粉碎，他们放火烧了工厂

they seek to restore by force the vanished status of the workman of the Middle Ages

他们试图用武力恢复中世纪工人消失的地位

At this stage the labourers still form an incoherent mass scattered over the whole country

在这个阶段，工人仍然形成一个分散在全国各地的不连贯的群众

and they are broken up by their mutual competition

他们因相互竞争而破裂

If anywhere they unite to form more compact bodies, this is not yet the consequence of their own active union

如果它们在任何地方联合起来形成更紧凑的机构，这还不是他们自己积极联合的结果

but it is a consequence of the union of the Bourgeoisie, to attain its own political ends

但这是资产阶级联合的结果，以达到自己的政治目的

the Bourgeoisie is compelled to set the whole Proletariat in motion

资产阶级被迫发动整个无产阶级的运动

and moreover, for a time being, the Bourgeoisie is able to do so

而且，暂时，资产阶级能够这样做

At this stage, therefore, the proletarians do not fight their enemies

因此，在这个阶段，无产者不与敌人作战

but instead they are fighting the enemies of their enemies

相反，他们正在与敌人的敌人作战

the fight the remnants of absolute monarchy and the landowners

与绝对君主制和地主的残余作斗争

they fight the non-industrial Bourgeoisie; the petty Bourgeoisie

他们与非工业资产阶级作斗争;小资产阶级

Thus the whole historical movement is concentrated in the hands of the Bourgeoisie

这样，整个历史运动就集中在资产阶级的手中

every victory so obtained is a victory for the Bourgeoisie

这样取得的每一场胜利，都是资产阶级的胜利

But with the development of industry the Proletariat not only increases in number

但是，随着工业的发展，无产阶级不仅在人数上有所增加

the Proletariat becomes concentrated in greater masses and its strength grows

无产阶级集中于更大的群众，无产阶级的力量在增长

and the Proletariat feels that strength more and more

无产阶级越来越感受到这种力量

The various interests and conditions of life within the ranks of the Proletariat are more and more equalised

无产阶级队伍中的各种利益和生活条件越来越平等

they become more in proportion as machinery obliterates all distinctions of labour

随着机器消除了所有劳动的区别，它们变得更加相称

and machinery nearly everywhere reduces wages to the same low level

几乎所有地方的机器都把工资降低到同样的低水平

The growing competition among the Bourgeoisie, and the resulting commercial crises, make the wages of the workers ever more fluctuating

资产阶级之间日益激烈的竞争，以及由此产生的商业危机，使工人的工资更加波动

The unceasing improvement of machinery, ever more rapidly developing, makes their livelihood more and more precarious

机器的不断改进，越来越迅速的发展，使他们的生计越来越不稳定

the collisions between individual workmen and individual

Bourgeoisie take more and more the character of collisions between two classes

个别工人和个别资产阶级之间的冲突越来越具有两个阶级之间冲突的性质

Thereupon the workers begin to form combinations (Trades Unions) against the Bourgeoisie

于是，工人开始结成反对资产阶级的联合体（工会）

they club together in order to keep up the rate of wages

他们为了保持工资水平而聚在一起

they found permanent associations in order to make provision beforehand for these occasional revolts

他们找到了永久的协会，以便事先为这些偶尔的叛乱做好准备

Here and there the contest breaks out into riots

比赛在这里和那里爆发了骚乱

Now and then the workers are victorious, but only for a time

工人们时不时地取得胜利，但只是暂时的

The real fruit of their battles lies, not in the immediate result, but in the ever-expanding union of the workers

他们斗争的真正成果不在于立竿见影的结果，而在于不断扩大的工人工会

This union is helped on by the improved means of communication that are created by modern industry

现代工业创造的改进的通信手段有助于这种结合

modern communication places the workers of different localities in contact with one another

现代通信使不同地区的工人相互联系

It was just this contact that was needed to centralise the numerous local struggles into one national struggle between classes

正是这种联系，才需要将众多的地方斗争集中到一个阶级之间的全国性斗争中来

all of these struggles are of the same character, and every class struggle is a political struggle

所有这些斗争都具有相同的性质，每一次阶级斗争都是政治斗争

the burghers of the Middle Ages, with their miserable highways, required centuries to form their unions

中世纪的市民，他们悲惨的高速公路，需要几个世纪才能组建他们的工会

the modern proletarians, thanks to railways, achieve their unions within a few years

现代无产者，多亏了铁路，在几年内就实现了工会

This organisation of the proletarians into a class consequently formed them into a political party

无产者组织成一个阶级，于是把他们组成了一个政党

the political class is continually being upset again by the competition between the workers themselves

政治阶层不断地被工人之间的竞争所困扰

But the political class continues to rise up again, stronger, firmer, mightier

但政治阶层继续再次崛起，更强大、更坚定、更强大

It compels legislative recognition of particular interests of the workers

它迫使立法承认工人的特殊利益

it does this by taking advantage of the divisions among the Bourgeoisie itself

它通过利用资产阶级本身的分裂来做到这一点

Thus the ten-hours' bill in England was put into law

因此，英国的十小时法案被纳入法律

in many ways the collisions between the classes of the old society further is the course of development of the Proletariat

在许多方面，旧社会各阶级之间的冲突是无产阶级发展的进程

The Bourgeoisie finds itself involved in a constant battle

资产阶级发现自己卷入了一场持续不断的战斗

At first it will find itself involved in a constant battle with the aristocracy

起初，它会发现自己卷入了与贵族的持续斗争

later on it will find itself involved in a constant battle with those portions of the Bourgeoisie itself

以后，它将发现自己卷入了与资产阶级本身的那些部分的不断斗争中

and their interests will have become antagonistic to the progress of industry

他们的利益将与工业的进步背道而驰

at all times, their interests will have become antagonistic with the Bourgeoisie of foreign countries

在任何时候，他们的利益都会与外国资产阶级对立

In all these battles it sees itself compelled to appeal to the Proletariat, and asks for its help

在所有这些斗争中，它认为自己不得不向无产阶级求助，并请求无产阶级的帮助

and thus, it will feel compelled to drag it into the political arena

因此，它将被迫将其拖入政治舞台

The Bourgeoisie itself, therefore, supplies the Proletariat with its own instruments of political and general education

因此，资产阶级本身就向无产阶级提供自己的政治和一般教育工具

in other words, it furnishes the Proletariat with weapons for fighting the Bourgeoisie

换言之，它为无产阶级提供了与资产阶级作斗争的武器

Further, as we have already seen, entire sections of the ruling classes are precipitated into the Proletariat

此外，正如我们已经看到的，统治阶级的整个部分都沉淀成无产阶级

the advance of industry sucks them into the Proletariat

工业的进步把他们吸进了无产阶级

or, at least, they are threatened in their conditions of existence

或者，至少，他们的生存条件受到威胁

These also supply the Proletariat with fresh elements of enlightenment and progress

这些也为无产阶级提供了启蒙和进步的新元素

Finally, in times when the class struggle nears the decisive hour

最后，在阶级斗争接近决定性时刻的时候

the process of dissolution going on within the ruling class

统治阶级内部正在进行的解体过程

in fact, the dissolution going on within the ruling class will be felt within the whole range of society

事实上，统治阶级内部的解体将在整个社会中感受到

it will take on such a violent, glaring character, that a small section of the ruling class cuts itself adrift

它将呈现出如此暴力、刺眼的特征，以至于统治阶级的一小部分人会漂泊不定

and that ruling class will join the revolutionary class

统治阶级将加入革命阶级

the revolutionary class being the class that holds the future in its hands

革命阶级是把未来掌握在自己手中的阶级

Just as at an earlier period, a section of the nobility went over to the Bourgeoisie

就像在更早的时期一样，一部分贵族倒向了资产阶级

the same way a portion of the Bourgeoisie will go over to the Proletariat

同样，一部分资产阶级将转向无产阶级

in particular, a portion of the Bourgeoisie will go over to a portion of the Bourgeoisie ideologists

特别是，一部分资产阶级将转向一部分资产阶级思想家

Bourgeoisie ideologists who have raised themselves to the level of comprehending theoretically the historical movement as a whole

资产阶级思想家，他们把自己提高到从理论上理解整个历史运动的水平

Of all the classes that stand face to face with the Bourgeoisie today, the Proletariat alone is a really revolutionary class

在今天与资产阶级面对面的所有阶级中，只有无产阶级是一个真正的革命阶级

The other classes decay and finally disappear in the face of Modern Industry

其他阶级在现代工业面前腐朽并最终消失

the Proletariat is its special and essential product

无产阶级是无产阶级的特殊和必不可少的产品

The lower middle class, the small manufacturer, the shopkeeper, the artisan, the peasant

下层中产阶级、小制造商、店主、工匠、农民

all these fight against the Bourgeoisie

所有这些都是反对资产阶级的

they fight as fractions of the middle class to save themselves from extinction
他们作为中产阶级的一部分而战，以拯救自己免于灭绝

They are therefore not revolutionary, but conservative
因此，他们不是革命的，而是保守的

Nay more, they are reactionary, for they try to roll back the wheel of history
更何况，他们是反动的，因为他们试图推翻历史的车轮

If by chance they are revolutionary, they are so only in view of their impending transfer into the Proletariat
如果说他们是革命的，那只是因为他们即将转入无产阶级

they thus defend not their present, but their future interests
因此，他们捍卫的不是他们现在的利益，而是他们未来的利益

they desert their own standpoint to place themselves at that of the Proletariat
他们抛弃了自己的立场，把自己置于无产阶级的立场上

The "dangerous class," the social scum, that passively rotting mass thrown off by the lowest layers of old society
"危险阶级"，社会败类，被旧社会最底层抛弃的被动腐烂的群众

they may, here and there, be swept into the movement by a proletarian revolution
他们可能会在这里和那里被无产阶级革命卷入运动

its conditions of life, however, prepare it far more for the part of a bribed tool of reactionary intrigue
然而，它的生活条件使它为反动阴谋的贿赂工具做好了更多的准备

In the conditions of the Proletariat, those of old society at large are already virtually swamped
在无产阶级的条件下，整个旧社会的状况实际上已经被淹没了

The proletarian is without property
无产者是没有财产的

his relation to his wife and children has no longer anything in common with the Bourgeoisie's family-relations
他与妻子和孩子的关系与资产阶级的家庭关系不再有任何共同之处

modern industrial labour, modern subjection to capital, the same in England as in France, in America as in Germany

现代工业劳动，现代对资本的服从，在英国和法国一样，在美国和德国一样

his condition in society has stripped him of every trace of national character

他在社会上的地位剥夺了他民族性格的每一丝痕迹

Law, morality, religion, are to him so many Bourgeoisie prejudices

法律、道德、宗教，对他来说是那么多的资产阶级偏见

and behind these prejudices lurk in ambush just as many Bourgeoisie interests

在这些偏见的背后，潜伏着许多资产阶级利益

All the preceding classes that got the upper hand, sought to fortify their already acquired status

所有先前占上风的阶级都试图巩固他们已经获得的地位

they did this by subjecting society at large to their conditions of appropriation

他们通过使整个社会服从他们的占有条件来做到这一点

The proletarians cannot become masters of the productive forces of society

无产者不能成为社会生产力的主人

it can only do this by abolishing their own previous mode of appropriation

它只能通过废除自己以前的拨款模式来做到这一点

and thereby it also abolishes every other previous mode of appropriation

因此，它也废除了以前的所有其他拨款方式

They have nothing of their own to secure and to fortify

他们没有自己的任何东西可以保护和加强

their mission is to destroy all previous securities for, and insurances of, individual property

他们的任务是销毁所有以前的个人财产证券和保险

All previous historical movements were movements of minorities

以前所有的历史运动都是少数民族的运动

or they were movements in the interests of minorities

或者它们是为了少数群体的利益而进行的运动

The proletarian movement is the self-conscious, independent movement of the immense majority

无产阶级运动是绝大多数人的自觉的、独立的运动

and it is a movement in the interests of the immense majority

这是一场符合绝大多数人利益的运动

The Proletariat, the lowest stratum of our present society

无产阶级，我们当今社会的最底层

it cannot stir or raise itself up without the whole superincumbent strata of official society being sprung into the air

如果没有官方社会的整个上层阶级，它就无法搅动或提升自己

Though not in substance, yet in form, the struggle of the Proletariat with the Bourgeoisie is at first a national struggle

无产阶级同资产阶级的斗争虽然不是实质上的，但形式上却是民族斗争

The Proletariat of each country must, of course, first of all settle matters with its own Bourgeoisie

当然，每个国家的无产阶级首先必须同自己的资产阶级解决问题

In depicting the most general phases of the development of the Proletariat, we traced the more or less veiled civil war

在描述无产阶级发展的最一般阶段时，我们追溯了或多或少隐蔽的内战

this civil is raging within existing society

这种民间在现存社会中肆虐

it will rage up to the point where that war breaks out into open revolution

它将肆虐到战争爆发为公开革命的地步

and then the violent overthrow of the Bourgeoisie lays the foundation for the sway of the Proletariat

然后暴力推翻资产阶级，为无产阶级的统治奠定了基础

Hitherto, every form of society has been based, as we have already seen, on the antagonism of oppressing and oppressed classes

正如我们已经看到的那样，迄今为止，每一种社会形式都是建

立在压迫阶级和被压迫阶级的对抗之上的

But in order to oppress a class, certain conditions must be assured to it

但是，为了压迫一个阶级，必须向它保证某些条件

the class must be kept under conditions in which it can, at least, continue its slavish existence

这个阶级必须保持在至少能够继续其奴隶存在的条件下

The serf, in the period of serfdom, raised himself to membership in the commune

农奴在农奴制时期，将自己提升为公社成员

just as the petty Bourgeoisie, under the yoke of feudal absolutism, managed to develop into a Bourgeoisie

正如小资产阶级在封建专制主义的枷锁下，设法发展成为资产阶级一样

The modern labourer, on the contrary, instead of rising with the progress of industry, sinks deeper and deeper

相反，现代劳动者不但没有随着工业的进步而上升，反而越陷越深

he sinks below the conditions of existence of his own class

他沉沦在自己阶级的生存条件之下

He becomes a pauper, and pauperism develops more rapidly than population and wealth

他变成了一个穷人，而穷人比人口和财富发展得更快

And here it becomes evident, that the Bourgeoisie is unfit any longer to be the ruling class in society

在这里，很明显，资产阶级不再适合成为社会的统治阶级

and it is unfit to impose its conditions of existence upon society as an over-riding law

不宜将其生存条件作为压倒一切的法律强加于社会

It is unfit to rule because it is incompetent to assure an existence to its slave within his slavery

它不适合统治，因为它没有能力确保它的奴隶在他的奴役中生存

because it cannot help letting him sink into such a state, that it has to feed him, instead of being fed by him

因为它忍不住让他陷入这样的状态，以至于它必须喂养他，而不是被他喂养

Society can no longer live under this Bourgeoisie
社会不能再生活在这种资产阶级的统治下

in other words, its existence is no longer compatible with society
换句话说，它的存在不再与社会相容

The essential condition for the existence, and for the sway of the Bourgeoisie class, is the formation and augmentation of capital
资产阶级存在和影响的必要条件是资本的形成和壮大

the condition for capital is wage-labour
资本的条件是雇佣劳动

Wage-labour rests exclusively on competition between the labourers
雇佣劳动完全建立在劳动者之间的竞争之上

The advance of industry, whose involuntary promoter is the Bourgeoisie, replaces the isolation of the labourers
工业的进步，其非自愿的推动者是资产阶级，它取代了工人的孤立

due to competition, due to their revolutionary combination, due to association
由于竞争，由于他们的革命性组合，由于协会

The development of Modern Industry cuts from under its feet the very foundation on which the Bourgeoisie produces and appropriates products
现代工业的发展，从脚下割断了资产阶级生产和占有产品的基础

What the Bourgeoisie produces, above all, is its own grave-diggers
资产阶级生产的，首先是它自己的掘墓人

The fall of the Bourgeoisie and the victory of the Proletariat are equally inevitable
资产阶级的垮台和无产阶级的胜利同样是不可避免的

Proletarians and Communists
无产者和共产主义者

In what relation do the Communists stand to the proletarians as a whole?
共产党人与整个无产者的关系是什么？

The Communists do not form a separate party opposed to other working-class parties
共产党人没有组成一个反对其他工人阶级政党的独立政党

They have no interests separate and apart from those of the proletariat as a whole
他们没有与整个无产阶级的利益分开的利益

They do not set up any sectarian principles of their own, by which to shape and mould the proletarian movement
他们没有建立自己的任何宗派原则来塑造和塑造无产阶级运动

The Communists are distinguished from the other working-class parties by only two things
共产党与其他工人阶级政党的区别仅在于两件事

Firstly, they point out and bring to the front the common interests of the entire proletariat, independently of all nationality
首先，他们指出并把整个无产阶级的共同利益摆在前面，不分民族

this they do in the national struggles of the proletarians of the different countries
他们在不同国家的无产阶级的民族斗争中就是这样做的

Secondly, they always and everywhere represent the interests of the movement as a whole
其次，他们无时无刻不在代表整个运动的利益

this they do in the various stages of development, which the struggle of the working class against the Bourgeoisie has to pass through
他们在工人阶级反对资产阶级的斗争必须经历的各个发展阶段中都是这样做的

The Communists, therefore, are on the one hand, practically, the most advanced and resolute section of the working-class parties of every country

因此，共产党人一方面实际上是各国工人阶级政党中最先进、最坚定的部分

they are that section of the working class which pushes forward all others

他们是工人阶级中推动所有其他阶级前进的那部分人

theoretically, they also have the advantage of clearly understanding the line of march

从理论上讲，它们还具有清楚地了解行军路线的优势

this they understand better compared the great mass of the proletariat

与无产阶级的广大群众相比，他们更了解这一点

they understand the conditions, and the ultimate general results of the proletarian movement

他们了解无产阶级运动的条件和最终的一般结果

The immediate aim of the Communist is the same as that of all the other proletarian parties

共产党的直接目标同所有其他无产阶级政党的直接目标相同

their aim is the formation of the proletariat into a class

他们的目标是把无产阶级形成一个阶级

they aim to overthrow the Bourgeoisie supremacy

他们的目标是推翻资产阶级至高无上的地位

the strive for the conquest of political power by the proletariat

无产阶级夺取政权的斗争

The theoretical conclusions of the Communists are in no way based on ideas or principles of reformers

共产党人的理论结论绝不是基于改革者的思想或原则

it wasn't would-be universal reformers that invented or discovered the theoretical conclusions of the Communists

发明或发现共产党人的理论结论的不是潜在的普遍改革者

They merely express, in general terms, actual relations springing from an existing class struggle

它们只是笼统地表达了从现存的阶级斗争中产生的实际关系

and they describe the historical movement going on under our very eyes that have created this class struggle

他们描述了在我们眼皮底下发生的历史运动，这些运动造成了这场阶级斗争

The abolition of existing property relations is not at all a
distinctive feature of Communism
废除现存的财产关系根本不是共产主义的一个显著特征
All property relations in the past have continually been
subject to historical change
过去的所有财产关系都不断受到历史变化的影响
and these changes were consequent upon the change in
historical conditions
这些变化是历史条件变化的结果
The French Revolution, for example, abolished feudal
property in favour of Bourgeoisie property
例如，法国大革命废除了封建财产，取而代之的是资产阶级财
产
The distinguishing feature of Communism is not the
abolition of property, generally
共产主义的显著特征不是废除财产
but the distinguishing feature of Communism is the
abolition of Bourgeoisie property
但共产主义的显著特点是废除了资产阶级财产
But modern Bourgeoisie private property is the final and
most complete expression of the system of producing and
appropriating products
但是，现代资产阶级私有制是生产和占有产品制度的最后和最
完整的表现
it is the final state of a system that is based on class
antagonisms, where class antagonism is the exploitation of
the many by the few
这是一个建立在阶级对立基础上的制度的最终状态，在这种制
度中，阶级对立是少数人对多数人的剥削
In this sense, the theory of the Communists may be summed
up in the single sentence; the Abolition of private property
从这个意义上说，共产党人的理论可以用一句话来概括;废除私
有财产
We Communists have been reproached with the desire of
abolishing the right of personally acquiring property
我们共产党人因废除个人获得财产的权利而受到指责
it is claimed that this property is the fruit of a man's own

labour

据称，这种财产是人类自己劳动的成果

and this property is alleged to be the groundwork of all personal freedom, activity and independence.

据称，这种财产是所有个人自由、活动和独立的基础。

"Hard-won, self-acquired, self-earned property!"

"来之不易的、自得的、自赚来的财产！"

Do you mean the property of the petty artisan and of the small peasant?

你是说小手工业者和小农的财产吗？

Do you mean a form of property that preceded the Bourgeoisie form?

你是说资产阶级形式之前的一种财产形式吗？

There is no need to abolish that, the development of industry has to a great extent already destroyed it

没有必要废除它，工业的发展在很大程度上已经摧毁了它

and development of industry is still destroying it daily

工业的发展每天都在摧毁它

Or do you mean modern Bourgeoisie private property?

或者你是说现代资产阶级的私有财产？

But does wage-labour create any property for the labourer?

但是，雇佣劳动能为劳动者创造任何财产吗？

no, wage labour creates not one bit of this kind of property!

不，雇佣劳动没有创造这种财产的一点点！

what wage labour does create is capital; that kind of property which exploits wage-labour

雇佣劳动创造的是资本;那种剥削雇佣劳动的财产

capital cannot increase except upon condition of begetting a new supply of wage-labour for fresh exploitation

资本不能增加，除非是产生新的雇佣劳动供给，以便进行新的剥削

Property, in its present form, is based on the antagonism of capital and wage-labour

目前形式的财产是建立在资本和雇佣劳动的对立之上的

Let us examine both sides of this antagonism

让我们来看看这种对立的双方

To be a capitalist is to have not only a purely personal status

成为资本家不仅要有纯粹的个人地位

instead, to be a capitalist is also to have a social status in production

相反，成为资本家也是在生产中具有社会地位

because capital is a collective product; only by the united action of many members can it be set in motion

因为资本是集体产品;只有通过许多成员的联合行动，它才能启动起来

but this united action is a last resort, and actually requires all members of society

但这种联合行动是最后的手段，实际上需要社会所有成员

Capital does get converted into the property of all members of society

资本确实转化为社会所有成员的财产

but Capital is, therefore, not a personal power; it is a social power

但因此，资本不是个人的力量;它是一种社会力量

so when capital is converted into social property, personal property is not thereby transformed into social property

因此，当资本转化为社会财产时，个人财产并没有因此转化为社会财产

It is only the social character of the property that is changed, and loses its class-character

只是财产的社会性质发生了变化，失去了它的阶级性质

Let us now look at wage-labour

现在让我们看看雇佣劳动

The average price of wage-labour is the minimum wage, i.e., that quantum of the means of subsistence

雇佣劳动的平均价格是最低工资，即生活资料的数量

this wage is absolutely requisite in bare existence as a labourer

这个工资对于作为劳动者来说是绝对必要的

What, therefore, the wage-labourer appropriates by means of his labour, merely suffices to prolong and reproduce a bare existence

因此，雇佣劳动者通过他的劳动所占有的东西，只够延长和再生产一种赤裸裸的生活

We by no means intend to abolish this personal
appropriation of the products of labour

我们决不打算废除这种对劳动产品的个人占有

an appropriation that is made for the maintenance and
reproduction of human life

为维持和繁衍人类生命而进行的拨款

such personal appropriation of the products of labour leave
no surplus wherewith to command the labour of others

这种个人对劳动产品的占有，没有留下任何剩余来支配别人的
劳动

All that we want to do away with, is the miserable character
of this appropriation

我们想要消除的只是这种挪用的悲惨性质

the appropriation under which the labourer lives merely to
increase capital

劳动者生活所依赖的占有只是为了增加资本

he is allowed to live only in so far as the interest of the
ruling class requires it

他只被允许在统治阶级的利益需要的范围内生活

In Bourgeoisie society, living labour is but a means to
increase accumulated labour

在资产阶级社会中，活劳动不过是增加积累劳动的手段

In Communist society, accumulated labour is but a means to
widen, to enrich, to promote the existence of the labourer

在共产主义社会中，积累的劳动只不过是扩大、丰富和促进劳
动者生存的手段

In Bourgeoisie society, therefore, the past dominates the
present

因此，在资产阶级社会中，过去支配着现在

in Communist society the present dominates the past

在共产主义社会中，现在主宰过去

In Bourgeoisie society capital is independent and has
individuality

在资产阶级社会中，资本是独立的，具有个性的

In Bourgeoisie society the living person is dependent and
has no individuality

在资产阶级社会中，活着的人是依赖的，没有个性

And the abolition of this state of things is called by the Bourgeoisie, abolition of individuality and freedom!

资产阶级把废除这种状况称为废除个性和自由！

And it is rightly called the abolition of individuality and freedom!

它被正确地称为废除个性和自由！

Communism aims for the abolition of Bourgeoisie individuality

共产主义的目标是消灭资产阶级的个性

Communism intends for the abolition of Bourgeoisie independence

共产主义打算废除资产阶级独立

Bourgeoisie freedom is undoubtedly what communism is aiming at

资产阶级自由无疑是共产主义的目标

under the present Bourgeoisie conditions of production, freedom means free trade, free selling and buying

在资产阶级目前的生产条件下，自由意味着自由贸易、自由买卖

But if selling and buying disappears, free selling and buying also disappears

但是，如果买卖消失了，那么自由买卖也消失了

"brave words" by the Bourgeoisie about free selling and buying only have meaning in a limited sense

资产阶级关于自由买卖的"勇敢的话"只在有限的意义上有意义

these words have meaning only in contrast with restricted selling and buying

这些词只有在与限制买卖形成对比时才有意义

and these words have meaning only when applied to the fettered traders of the Middle Ages

这些词只有在应用于中世纪受束缚的商人时才有意义

and that assumes these words even have meaning in a Bourgeoisie sense

这就假定这些词在资产阶级的意义上甚至有意义

but these words have no meaning when they're being used to oppose the Communistic abolition of buying and selling

但是，当这些词被用来反对共产主义废除买卖时，它们就没有

任何意义了

the words have no meaning when they're being used to oppose the Bourgeoisie conditions of production being abolished

当这些词被用来反对废除资产阶级生产条件时，它们就没有意义了

and they have no meaning when they're being used to oppose the Bourgeoisie itself being abolished

当它们被用来反对资产阶级本身被废除时，它们就没有任何意义了

You are horrified at our intending to do away with private property

你对我们打算废除私有财产感到震惊

But in your existing society, private property is already done away with for nine-tenths of the population

但是在你们现有的社会中，十分之九的人口已经废除了私有财产

the existence of private property for the few is solely due to its non-existence in the hands of nine-tenths of the population

少数人的私有财产之所以存在，完全是因为私有财产在十分之九的人口手中不存在

You reproach us, therefore, with intending to do away with a form of property

因此，你责备我们打算废除一种财产形式

but private property necessitates the non-existence of any property for the immense majority of society

但是私有财产要求社会绝大多数人不存在任何财产

In one word, you reproach us with intending to do away with your property

一句话，你责备我们打算废除你的财产

And it is precisely so; doing away with your Property is just what we intend

事实正是如此;取消您的财产正是我们的意图

From the moment when labour can no longer be converted into capital, money, or rent

从劳动不能再转化为资本、货币或地租的那一刻起

when labour can no longer be converted into a social power capable of being monopolised

当劳动不能再转化为能够被垄断的社会力量时

from the moment when individual property can no longer be transformed into Bourgeoisie property

从个人财产不能再转化为资产阶级财产的那一刻起

from the moment when individual property can no longer be transformed into capital

从个人财产不能再转化为资本的那一刻起

from that moment, you say individuality vanishes

从那一刻起，你说个性消失了

You must, therefore, confess that by "individual" you mean no other person than the Bourgeoisie

因此，你必须承认，你所说的"个人"，除了资产阶级之外，不是指其他人

you must confess it specifically refers to the middle-class owner of property

你必须承认，它特指中产阶级的财产所有者

This person must, indeed, be swept out of the way, and made impossible

事实上，这个人必须被扫地出门，变得不可能

Communism deprives no man of the power to appropriate the products of society

共产主义不剥夺任何人占有社会产品的权力

all that Communism does is to deprive him of the power to subjugate the labour of others by means of such appropriation

共产主义所做的一切，就是剥夺他通过这种占有来征服他人劳动的权力

It has been objected that upon the abolition of private property all work will cease

有人反对说，一旦废除私有财产，所有工作都将停止

and it is then suggested that universal laziness will overtake us

然后有人建议普遍的懒惰将超越我们

According to this, Bourgeoisie society ought long ago to have gone to the dogs through sheer idleness

据此，资产阶级社会早就应该通过纯粹的懒惰去找狗了
because those of its members who work, acquire nothing
因为那些工作的成员，一无所获

and those of its members who acquire anything, do not work
而那些获得任何东西的成员，则不起作用

The whole of this objection is but another expression of the tautology
这种反对意见的全部不过是重言式的另一种表现形式

there can no longer be any wage-labour when there is no longer any capital
当不再有任何资本时，就不再有任何雇佣劳动

there is no difference between material products and mental products
物质产品和精神产品之间没有区别

communism proposes both of these are produced in the same way
共产主义提出这两者都是以同样的方式产生的

but the objections against the Communistic modes of producing these are the same
但是反对共产主义生产这些产品的方式是一样的

to the Bourgeoisie the disappearance of class property is the disappearance of production itself
对资产阶级来说，阶级财产的消失就是生产本身的消失

so the disappearance of class culture is to him identical with the disappearance of all culture
因此，在他看来，阶级文化的消失与所有文化的消失是一样的

That culture, the loss of which he laments, is for the enormous majority a mere training to act as a machine
他为这种文化的丧失而感到遗憾，对绝大多数人来说，仅仅是一种充当机器的训练

Communists very much intend to abolish the culture of Bourgeoisie property
共产党人非常打算废除资产阶级财产文化

But don't wrangle with us so long as you apply the standard of your Bourgeoisie notions of freedom, culture, law, etc
但是，只要你运用你的资产阶级自由、文化、法律等概念的标准，就不要和我们争吵

Your very ideas are but the outgrowth of the conditions of your Bourgeoisie production and Bourgeoisie property

你们的思想只不过是你们的资产阶级生产条件和资产阶级财产的产物

just as your jurisprudence is but the will of your class made into a law for all

正如你们的法理学只不过是你们阶级的意志成为所有人的法律一样

the essential character and direction of this will are determined by the economical conditions your social class create

这种意志的本质特征和方向是由你的社会阶层创造的经济条件决定的

The selfish misconception that induces you to transform social forms into eternal laws of nature and of reason

自私的误解，诱使你把社会形式转化为永恒的自然法则和理性法则

the social forms springing from your present mode of production and form of property

从你们现在的生产方式和财产形式中产生的社会形式

historical relations that rise and disappear in the progress of production

在生产过程中兴起和消失的历史关系

this misconception you share with every ruling class that has preceded you

你与你之前的每一个统治阶级都有这种误解

What you see clearly in the case of ancient property, what you admit in the case of feudal property

在古代财产的情况下，你清楚地看到的，在封建财产的情况下，你承认的

these things you are of course forbidden to admit in the case of your own Bourgeoisie form of property

在你自己的资产阶级财产形式的情况下，你当然是被禁止承认的

Abolition of the family! Even the most radical flare up at this infamous proposal of the Communists

废除家庭！即使是最激进的人也对共产党人的这个臭名昭著的

提议大发雷霆

On what foundation is the present family, the Bourgeoisie family, based?

现在的家庭，资产阶级家庭，是建立在什么基础上的？

the foundation of the present family is based on capital and private gain

目前家庭的基础是建立在资本和私人利益的基础上的

In its completely developed form this family exists only among the Bourgeoisie

在完全发展的形式中，这个家庭只存在于资产阶级中

this state of things finds its complement in the practical absence of the family among the proletarians

这种状况在无产者中家庭的实际缺席中得到了补充

this state of things can be found in public prostitution

这种状况可以在公开卖淫中找到

The Bourgeoisie family will vanish as a matter of course when its complement vanishes

当资产阶级家族的补充消失时，资产阶级家族将理所当然地消失

and both of these will will vanish with the vanishing of capital

而这两种意志都将随着资本的消失而消失

Do you charge us with wanting to stop the exploitation of children by their parents?

你是否指责我们想要阻止父母对儿童的剥削？

To this crime we plead guilty

对于这一罪行，我们认罪

But, you will say, we destroy the most hallowed of relations, when we replace home education by social education

但是，你会说，当我们用社会教育取代家庭教育时，我们破坏了最神圣的关系

is your education not also social? And is it not determined by the social conditions under which you educate?

你的教育不是也是社会的吗？这难道不是由你教育的社会条件决定的吗？

by the intervention, direct or indirect, of society, by means of schools, etc.

通过社会的直接或间接干预，通过学校等。

The Communists have not invented the intervention of society in education

共产党人没有发明社会对教育的干预

they do but seek to alter the character of that intervention

他们这样做只是试图改变这种干预的性质

and they seek to rescue education from the influence of the ruling class

他们试图将教育从统治阶级的影响中拯救出来

The Bourgeoisie talk of the hallowed co-relation of parent and child

资产阶级谈论父母和孩子的神圣关系

but this clap-trap about the family and education becomes all the more disgusting when we look at Modern Industry

但是，当我们看到现代工业时，这种关于家庭和教育的鼓掌陷阱变得更加令人作呕

all family ties among the proletarians are torn asunder by modern industry

无产者之间的一切家庭关系都被现代工业撕裂了

their children are transformed into simple articles of commerce and instruments of labour

他们的孩子变成了简单的商业物品和劳动工具

But you Communists would create a community of women, screams the whole Bourgeoisie in chorus

但是你们共产党人会创建一个妇女社区，让整个资产阶级齐声尖叫

The Bourgeoisie sees in his wife a mere instrument of production

资产阶级在妻子身上看到的只是生产工具

He hears that the instruments of production are to be exploited by all

他听说生产工具要被所有人利用

and, naturally, he can come to no other conclusion than that the lot of being common to all will likewise fall to women

而且，自然，他只能得出其他结论，即所有人共同的命运同样会落在女人身上

He has not even a suspicion that the real point is to do away

with the status of women as mere instruments of production
他甚至没有怀疑真正的意义在于消除妇女作为生产工具的地位

For the rest, nothing is more ridiculous than the virtuous indignation of our Bourgeoisie at the community of women
至于其余的，没有什么比我们资产阶级对妇女社区的道德愤慨更荒谬的了

they pretend it is to be openly and officially established by the Communists
他们假装这是共产党人公开和正式建立的

The Communists have no need to introduce community of women, it has existed almost from time immemorial
共产党人没有必要引入妇女社区，它几乎从远古时代就存在

Our Bourgeoisie are not content with having the wives and daughters of their proletarians at their disposal
我们的资产阶级不满足于拥有无产者的妻子和女儿

they take the greatest pleasure in seducing each other's wives
他们以勾引对方的妻子为乐

and that is not even to speak of common prostitutes
这甚至不是普通

Bourgeoisie marriage is in reality a system of wives in common
资产阶级婚姻实际上是一种共同的妻子制度

then there is one thing that the Communists might possibly be reproached with
那么有一件事共产党人可能会受到指责

they desire to introduce an openly legalised community of women
他们希望引入一个公开合法化的妇女社区

rather than a hypocritically concealed community of women
而不是一个虚伪隐藏的女性社区

the community of women springing from the system of production
从生产体系中产生的妇女社区

abolish the system of production, and you abolish the community of women
廢除生產制度，你就廢除婦女社區

both public prostitution is abolished, and private prostitution

公开卖淫和私人卖淫都被废除了

The Communists are further more reproached with desiring to abolish countries and nationality

共产党人更是想废除国家和民族

The working men have no country, so we cannot take from them what they have not got

工人没有国家，所以我们不能从他们那里拿走他们没有得到的东西

the proletariat must first of all acquire political supremacy

无产阶级首先必须获得政治上的至高无上的地位

the proletariat must rise to be the leading class of the nation

无产阶级必须成为国家的领导阶级

the proletariat must constitute itself the nation

无产阶级必须把自己建成民族

it is, so far, itself national, though not in the Bourgeoisie sense of the word

到目前为止，它本身是民族的，尽管不是资产阶级意义上的

National differences and antagonisms between peoples are daily more and more vanishing

民族差异和民族之间的对立日益消失

owing to the development of the Bourgeoisie, to freedom of commerce, to the world-market

由于资产阶级的发展，由于商业自由，由于世界市场

to uniformity in the mode of production and in the conditions of life corresponding thereto

生产方式和与之相适应的生活条件的统一性

The supremacy of the proletariat will cause them to vanish still faster

无产阶级的至高无上地位将使他们消失得更快

United action, of the leading civilised countries at least, is one of the first conditions for the emancipation of the proletariat

至少是主要文明国家的联合行动，是无产阶级解放的首要条件之一

In proportion as the exploitation of one individual by

another is put an end to, the exploitation of one nation by another will also be put an end to

随着一个人对另一个人的剥削被结束，一个国家对另一个国家的剥削也将被结束。

In proportion as the antagonism between classes within the nation vanishes, the hostility of one nation to another will come to an end

随着国家内部阶级之间的对立消失，一个国家对另一个国家的敌意将相应结束

The charges against Communism made from a religious, a philosophical, and, generally, from an ideological standpoint, are not deserving of serious examination

从宗教、哲学和一般意识形态的角度对共产主义的指控不值得认真研究

Does it require deep intuition to comprehend that man's ideas, views and conceptions changes with every change in the conditions of his material existence?

难道需要深刻的直觉才能理解人的思想、观点和观念随着物质生存条件的每一次变化而变化吗？

is it not obvious that man's consciousness changes when his social relations and his social life changes?

当人的社会关系和社会生活发生变化时，人的意识会发生变化，这难道不是显而易见的吗？

What else does the history of ideas prove, than that intellectual production changes its character in proportion as material production is changed?

思想史除了证明知识生产随着物质生产的变化而成比例地改变其性质之外，还有什么呢？

The ruling ideas of each age have ever been the ideas of its ruling class

每个时代的统治思想都是其统治阶级的思想

When people speak of ideas that revolutionise society, they do but express one fact

当人们谈论彻底改变社会的想法时，他们只表达了一个事实

within the old society, the elements of a new one have been created

在旧社会中，新社会的元素已经产生

and that the dissolution of the old ideas keeps even pace with the dissolution of the old conditions of existence

旧观念的消解与旧存在条件的消解保持同步

When the ancient world was in its last throes, the ancient religions were overcome by Christianity

当古代世界处于最后的阵痛中时，古老的宗教被基督教所征服

When Christian ideas succumbed in the 18th century to rationalist ideas, feudal society fought its death battle with the then revolutionary Bourgeoisie

当基督教思想在18世纪屈服于理性主义思想时，封建社会与当时的革命资产阶级进行了殊死搏斗

The ideas of religious liberty and freedom of conscience merely gave expression to the sway of free competition within the domain of knowledge

宗教自由和良心自由的思想只是表达了知识领域内自由竞争的影响力

"Undoubtedly," it will be said, "religious, moral, philosophical and juridical ideas have been modified in the course of historical development"

"毫无疑问，"人们会说，"宗教、道德、哲学和法律观念在历史发展过程中发生了变化"

"But religion, morality philosophy, political science, and law, constantly survived this change"

"但宗教、道德哲学、政治学和法律，不断在这种变化中幸存下来"

"There are also eternal truths, such as Freedom, Justice, etc"

"还有永恒的真理，如自由、正义等"

"these eternal truths are common to all states of society"

"这些永恒的真理是所有社会状态的共同真理"

"But Communism abolishes eternal truths, it abolishes all religion, and all morality"

"但共产主义废除了永恒的真理，它废除了所有的宗教和所有的道德"

"it does this instead of constituting them on a new basis"

"它这样做，而不是在新的基础上构成它们"

"it therefore acts in contradiction to all past historical experience"

"因此，它的行为与过去的所有历史经验相矛盾"

What does this accusation reduce itself to?

这种指责本身归结为什么？

The history of all past society has consisted in the development of class antagonisms

过去所有社会的历史都是在阶级对立的发展中形成的

antagonisms that assumed different forms at different epochs

在不同时代呈现不同形式的对立

But whatever form they may have taken, one fact is common to all past ages

但无论他们采取何种形式，一个事实是过去所有时代的共同事实

the exploitation of one part of society by the other

社会的一部分被另一部分剥削

No wonder, then, that the social consciousness of past ages moves within certain common forms, or general ideas

因此，难怪过去时代的社会意识是在某些共同的形式或一般观念中运动的

(and that is despite all the multiplicity and variety it displays)

（尽管它显示了所有的多样性和多样性）

and these cannot completely vanish except with the total disappearance of class antagonisms

除非阶级对立完全消失，否则这些都不可能完全消失

The Communist revolution is the most radical rupture with traditional property relations

共产主义革命是与传统财产关系最彻底的决裂

no wonder that its development involves the most radical rupture with traditional ideas

难怪它的发展涉及与传统观念的最彻底的决裂

But let us have done with the Bourgeoisie objections to Communism

但是，让我们把资产阶级对共产主义的反对说完了

We have seen above the first step in the revolution by the working class

我们已经看到了工人阶级革命的第一步

proletariat has to be raised to the position of ruling, to win the battle of democracy

无产阶级必须上升到统治的地位，才能赢得民主的战斗

The proletariat will use its political supremacy to wrest, by degrees, all capital from the Bourgeoisie

无产阶级将利用自己的政治优势，逐步从资产阶级手中夺取一切资本

it will centralise all instruments of production in the hands of the State

它将把所有生产工具集中在国家手中

in other words, the proletariat organised as the ruling class

换言之，无产阶级组织起来就是统治阶级

and it will increase the total of productive forces as rapidly as possible

它将尽快增加生产力总量

Of course, in the beginning, this cannot be effected except by means of despotic inroads on the rights of property

当然，在一开始，除非通过对财产权的专制干涉，否则这是无法实现的

and it has to be achieved on the conditions of Bourgeoisie production

它必须在资产阶级生产的条件下实现

it is achieved by means of measures, therefore, which appear economically insufficient and untenable

因此，它是通过在经济上似乎不足和站不住脚的措施来实现的

but these means, in the course of the movement, outstrip themselves

但是，在运动过程中，这些手段超越了自己

they necessitate further inroads upon the old social order

它们需要进一步侵入旧的社会秩序

and they are unavoidable as a means of entirely revolutionising the mode of production

它们作为彻底改变生产方式的手段是不可避免的

These measures will of course be different in different countries

当然，这些措施在不同的国家会有所不同

Nevertheless in the most advanced countries, the following

will be pretty generally applicable
然而，在最先进的国家，以下内容将非常普遍适用

1. Abolition of property in land and application of all rents of land to public purposes.
1.废除土地财产，将所有土地租金用于公共目的。

2. A heavy progressive or graduated income tax.
2. 重度累进或累进所得税。

3. Abolition of all right of inheritance.
3.废除一切继承权。

4. Confiscation of the property of all emigrants and rebels.
4. 没收所有移民和叛乱分子的财产。

5. Centralisation of credit in the hands of the State, by means of a national bank with State capital and an exclusive monopoly.
5.通过拥有国家资本和独家垄断的国家银行，将信贷集中到国家手中。

6. Centralisation of the means of communication and transport in the hands of the State.
6.通讯和运输手段集中于国家手中。

7. Extension of factories and instruments of production owned by the State
7.扩大国有工厂和生产工具

the bringing into cultivation of waste-lands, and the improvement of the soil generally in accordance with a common plan.
将荒地开垦开垦，并按照共同计划对土壤进行改良。

8. Equal liability of all to labour
8. 人人对劳动负有同等责任

Establishment of industrial armies, especially for agriculture.
建立工业军队，特别是农业军队。

9. Combination of agriculture with manufacturing industries
9. 农业与制造业的结合

gradual abolition of the distinction between town and country, by a more equable distribution of the population over the country.
逐步消除城乡的区别，在全国范围内更公平地分配人口。

10. Free education for all children in public schools.
10. 公立学校所有儿童均免费接受教育。

Abolition of children's factory labour in its present form
废除目前形式的工厂童工

Combination of education with industrial production
教育与工业生产相结合

When, in the course of development, class distinctions have disappeared
在发展过程中，阶级差异消失了

and when all production has been concentrated in the hands of a vast association of the whole nation
当所有生产都集中在整个民族的广大联合手中时

then the public power will lose its political character
那么公共权力将失去其政治性质

Political power, properly so called, is merely the organised power of one class for oppressing another
政治权力，恰如其分地称为政治权力，只是一个阶级压迫另一个阶级的有组织的力量

If the proletariat during its contest with the Bourgeoisie is compelled, by the force of circumstances, to organise itself as a class
如果无产阶级在与资产阶级的较量中，由于环境的力量，被迫把自己组织成一个阶级

if, by means of a revolution, it makes itself the ruling class
如果通过革命，它使自己成为统治阶级

and, as such, it sweeps away by force the old conditions of production
因此，它用武力扫除旧的生产条件

then it will, along with these conditions, have swept away the conditions for the existence of class antagonisms and of classes generally
这样，它就会同这些条件一起扫除阶级对立和一般阶级存在的条件

and will thereby have abolished its own supremacy as a class.
从而将废除它自己作为一个阶级的至高无上的地位。

In place of the old Bourgeoisie society, with its classes and

class antagonisms, we shall have an association
代替旧的资产阶级社会，它的阶级和阶级对立，我们将有一个联合体

an association in which the free development of each is the condition for the free development of all
一个协会，在这个协会中，每个人的自由发展是所有人自由发展的条件

a) Feudal Socialism
a) 封建社会主义

the aristocracies of France and England had a unique historical position
法国和英国的贵族具有独特的历史地位

it became their vocation to write pamphlets against modern Bourgeoisie society
写反对现代资产阶级社会的小册子成为他们的天职

In the French revolution of July 1830, and in the English reform agitation
在1830年7月的法国大革命和英国的改革鼓动中

these aristocracies again succumbed to the hateful upstart
这些贵族再次屈服于可恶的暴发户

Thenceforth, a serious political contest was altogether out of the question
从此以后，一场严肃的政治较量就完全不可能了

All that remained possible was literary battle, not an actual battle
剩下的只是文学之战，而不是一场真正的战斗

But even in the domain of literature the old cries of the restoration period had become impossible
但即使在文学领域，复辟时期的旧呼声也变得不可能了

In order to arouse sympathy, the aristocracy were obliged to lose sight, apparently, of their own interests
为了引起同情，贵族们显然不得不忽视自己的利益

and they were obliged to formulate their indictment against the Bourgeoisie in the interest of the exploited working class
他们不得不为了被剥削的工人阶级的利益而对资产阶级提出控诉

Thus the aristocracy took their revenge by singing lampoons on their new master
因此，贵族们通过对他们的新主人进行嘲讽来报复

and they took their revenge by whispering in his ears

sinister prophecies of coming catastrophe
他们为了报复，在他耳边低语着即将到来的灾难的险恶预言
In this way arose Feudal Socialism: half lamentation, half lampoon
封建社会主义就这样出现了：一半是哀叹，一半是嘲讽
it rung as half echo of the past, and projected half menace of the future
它一半是过去的回声，一半是未来的威胁
at times, by its bitter, witty and incisive criticism, it struck the Bourgeoisie to the very heart's core
有时，它以尖锐、诙谐和尖锐的批评，击中了资产阶级的核心
but it was always ludicrous in its effect, through total incapacity to comprehend the march of modern history
但它的效果总是荒谬的，因为它完全无法理解现代历史的进程
The aristocracy, in order to rally the people to them, waved the proletarian alms-bag in front for a banner
贵族们为了把人民团结到他们身边，在前面挥舞着无产阶级的施舍袋，要一面旗帜
But the people, so often as it joined them, saw on their hindquarters the old feudal coats of arms
但是，当它加入他们时，人们经常在他们的后躯上看到旧的封建纹章
and they deserted with loud and irreverent laughter
他们带着响亮而不敬的笑声离开了
One section of the French Legitimists and "Young England" exhibited this spectacle
一部分法国合法主义者和"年轻的英格兰"展示了这种奇观
the feudalists pointed out that their mode of exploitation was different to that of the Bourgeoisie
封建主义者指出，他们的剥削方式与资产阶级不同
the feudalists forget that they exploited under circumstances and conditions that were quite different
封建主义者忘记了他们在完全不同的环境和条件下进行剥削
and they didn't notice such methods of exploitation are now antiquated
他们没有注意到这种剥削方法现在已经过时了
they showed that, under their rule, the modern proletariat

never existed
他们表明，在他们的统治下，现代无产阶级从未存在过
but they forget that the modern Bourgeoisie is the necessary
offspring of their own form of society
但是他们忘记了现代资产阶级是他们自己社会形式的必要后代
For the rest, they hardly conceal the reactionary character of
their criticism
其余的，他们几乎不掩饰他们批评的反动性质
their chief accusation against the Bourgeoisie amounts to the
following
他们对资产阶级的主要指控如下
under the Bourgeoisie regime a social class is being
developed
在资产阶级政权下，一个社会阶级正在发展
this social class is destined to cut up root and branch the old
order of society
这个社会阶层注定要把社会的旧秩序连根拔起
What they upbraid the Bourgeoisie with is not so much that
it creates a proletariat
他们用什么来培养资产阶级，与其说是它创造了一个无产阶级
what they upbraid the Bourgeoisie with is moreso that it
creates a revolutionary proletariat
他们用什么来鼓舞资产阶级，更是为了它创造一个革命的无产
阶级
In political practice, therefore, they join in all coercive
measures against the working class
因此，在政治实践中，他们加入了一切针对工人阶级的强制措
施
and in ordinary life, despite their highfalutin phrases, they
stoop to pick up the golden apples dropped from the tree of
industry
而在平凡的生活中，尽管他们说着高调的短语，但他们还是弯
腰捡起从工业树上掉下来的金苹果
and they barter truth, love, and honour for commerce in
wool, beetroot-sugar, and potato spirits
他们用真理、爱和荣誉来换取羊毛、甜菜根糖和马铃薯烈酒的
商业

As the parson has ever gone hand in hand with the landlord, so has Clerical Socialism with Feudal Socialism

正如教区长与地主同来是相辅相成的，教士社会主义与封建社会主义同来也是同来的

Nothing is easier than to give Christian asceticism a Socialist tinge

没有什么比赋予基督教禁欲主义社会主义色彩更容易的了

Has not Christianity declaimed against private property, against marriage, against the State?

基督教不是反对私有财产，反对婚姻，反对国家吗？

Has Christianity not preached in the place of these, charity and poverty?

难道基督教没有代替这些，慈善和贫穷吗？

Does Christianity not preach celibacy and mortification of the flesh, monastic life and Mother Church?

难道基督教不宣扬独身和肉体、修道院生活和母教会的克制吗？

Christian Socialism is but the holy water with which the priest consecrates the heart-burnings of the aristocrat

基督教社会主义只不过是神父奉献贵族心灵燃烧的圣水

b) Petty-Bourgeois Socialism
b) 小资产阶级社会主义

The feudal aristocracy was not the only class that was ruined by the Bourgeoisie
封建贵族并不是唯一被资产阶级摧毁的阶级

it was not the only class whose conditions of existence pined and perished in the atmosphere of modern Bourgeoisie society
它并不是唯一一个在现代资产阶级社会的气氛中生存条件被钉住并消亡的阶级

The medieval burgesses and the small peasant proprietors were the precursors of the modern Bourgeoisie
中世纪的市民和小农主是现代资产阶级的先驱

In those countries which are but little developed, industrially and commercially, these two classes still vegetate side by side
在那些在工业和商业上都不太发达的国家，这两个阶级仍然并存

and in the meantime the Bourgeoisie rise up next to them: industrially, commercially, and politically
与此同时，资产阶级在他们旁边崛起：在工业上、商业上和政治上

In countries where modern civilisation has become fully developed, a new class of petty Bourgeoisie has been formed
在现代文明充分发展的国家，形成了新的小资产阶级阶级

this new social class fluctuates between proletariat and Bourgeoisie
这个新的社会阶级在无产阶级和资产阶级之间波动

and it is ever renewing itself as a supplementary part of Bourgeoisie society
它作为资产阶级社会的补充部分不断更新自己

The individual members of this class, however, are being constantly hurled down into the proletariat
然而，这个阶级的个别成员却不断地被扔到无产阶级中去

they are sucked up by the proletariat through the action of competition

他们被无产阶级通过竞争的作用吸走了

as modern industry develops they even see the moment
approaching when they will completely disappear as an
independent section of modern society

随着现代工业的发展，他们甚至看到了他们作为现代社会的一
个独立部分完全消失的时刻即将到来

they will be replaced, in manufactures, agriculture and
commerce, by overlookers, bailiffs and shopmen

在制造业、农业和商业领域，他们将被监督员、法警和店员所
取代

In countries like France, where the peasants constitute far
more than half of the population

在法国这样的国家，农民占人口的一半以上

it was natural that there there are writers who sided with the
proletariat against the Bourgeoisie

很自然地，有些作家站在无产阶级一边反对资产阶级

in their criticism of the Bourgeoisie regime they used the
standard of the peasant and petty Bourgeoisie

在对资产阶级政权的批评中，他们使用了农民和小资产阶级的
标准

and from the standpoint of these intermediate classes they
take up the cudgels for the working class

从这些中间阶级的立场来看，他们拿起了工人阶级的棍棒

Thus arose petty-Bourgeoisie Socialism, of which Sismondi
was the head of this school, not only in France but also in
England

于是出现了小资产阶级社会主义，西斯蒙第是这所学校的负责
人，不仅在法国，而且在英国

This school of Socialism dissected with great acuteness the
contradictions in the conditions of modern production

这个社会主义学派非常敏锐地剖析了现代生产条件中的矛盾

This school laid bare the hypocritical apologies of
economists

这所学校揭露了经济学家虚伪的道歉

This school proved, incontrovertibly, the disastrous effects
of machinery and division of labour

这所学校无可争辩地证明了机器和劳动分工的灾难性影响

it proved the concentration of capital and land in a few hands

它证明了资本和土地集中在少数人手中

it proved how overproduction leads to Bourgeoisie crises

它证明了生产过剩如何导致资产阶级危机

it pointed out the inevitable ruin of the petty Bourgeoisie and peasant

它指出了小资产阶级和农民的不可避免的毁灭

the misery of the proletariat, the anarchy in production, the crying inequalities in the distribution of wealth

无产阶级的苦难，生产中的无政府状态，财富分配中的不平等

it showed how the system of production leads the industrial war of extermination between nations

它展示了生产体系如何导致国家之间的工业灭绝战争

the dissolution of old moral bonds, of the old family relations, of the old nationalities

旧的道德纽带、旧的家庭关系、旧的民族的解体

In its positive aims, however, this form of Socialism aspires to achieve one of two things

然而，就其积极目标而言，这种形式的社会主义渴望实现两件事之一

either it aims to restore the old means of production and of exchange

它的目标是恢复旧的生产方式和交换方式

and with the old means of production it would restore the old property relations, and the old society

有了旧的生产资料，它就会恢复旧的财产关系和旧社会

or it aims to cramp the modern means of production and exchange into the old framework of the property relations

或者它旨在将现代生产和交换手段限制在财产关系的旧框架中

In either case, it is both reactionary and Utopian

无论哪种情况，它都是反动的和乌托邦的

Its last words are: corporate guilds for manufacture, patriarchal relations in agriculture

它的最后一句话是：制造业的公司行会，农业中的父权关系

Ultimately, when stubborn historical facts had dispersed all intoxicating effects of self-deception

最终，当顽固的历史事实驱散了所有自欺欺人的醉人影响时
this form of Socialism ended in a miserable fit of pity
这种形式的社会主义以悲惨的怜悯告终

c) German, or "True," Socialism
c) 德国的，或"真正的"社会主义

The Socialist and Communist literature of France originated under the pressure of a Bourgeoisie in power
法国的社会主义和共产主义文学起源于当权资产阶级的压力

and this literature was the expression of the struggle against this power
这种文学是与这种力量斗争的表达

it was introduced into Germany at a time when the Bourgeoisie had just begun its contest with feudal absolutism
它是在资产阶级刚刚开始与封建专制主义的斗争时引入德国的

German philosophers, would-be philosophers, and beaux esprits, eagerly seized on this literature
德国哲学家、未来的哲学家和美女们都热切地抓住了这些文献

but they forgot that the writings immigrated from France into Germany without bringing the French social conditions along
但他们忘记了，这些著作是从法国移民到德国的，并没有带来法国的社会状况

In contact with German social conditions, this French literature lost all its immediate practical significance
在与德国社会条件的接触中，这种法国文学失去了所有直接的现实意义

and the Communist literature of France assumed a purely literary aspect in German academic circles
法国的共产主义文学在德国学术界呈现出纯粹的文学一面

Thus, the demands of the first French Revolution were nothing more than the demands of "Practical Reason"
因此，第一次法国大革命的要求只不过是"实践理性"的要求

and the utterance of the will of the revolutionary French Bourgeoisie signified in their eyes the law of pure Will
在他们眼中，革命的法国资产阶级的意志的表达标志着纯粹意志的法则

it signified Will as it was bound to be; of true human Will generally

它象征着意志的必然;一般而言，真正的人类意志

The world of the German literati consisted solely in bringing the new French ideas into harmony with their ancient philosophical conscience

德国文人的世界完全在于使新的法国思想与他们古老的哲学良知相协调

or rather, they annexed the French ideas without deserting their own philosophic point of view

或者更确切地说，他们吞并了法国的思想，而没有放弃自己的哲学观点

This annexation took place in the same way in which a foreign language is appropriated, namely, by translation

这种兼并的发生方式与挪用外语的方式相同，即通过翻译

It is well known how the monks wrote silly lives of Catholic Saints over manuscripts

众所周知，僧侣们是如何在手稿上写下天主教圣徒的愚蠢生活

the manuscripts on which the classical works of ancient heathendom had been written

写有古代异教经典著作的手稿

The German literati reversed this process with the profane French literature

德国文人用亵渎的法国文学扭转了这一过程

They wrote their philosophical nonsense beneath the French original

他们在法国原版下面写下了他们的哲学废话

For instance, beneath the French criticism of the economic functions of money, they wrote "Alienation of Humanity"

例如，在法国对货币经济功能的批评之下，他们写了《人类的异化》

beneath the French criticism of the Bourgeoisie State they wrote "dethronement of the Category of the General"

在法国对资产阶级国家的批评之下，他们写下了"将军类别的废黜"

The introduction of these philosophical phrases at the back of the French historical criticisms they dubbed:

在法国历史批评的背后引入这些哲学短语，他们称之为：

"Philosophy of Action," "True Socialism," "German Science

of Socialism," "Philosophical Foundation of Socialism," and so on

《行动哲学》《真正的社会主义》《德国社会主义科学》《社会主义的哲学基础》等等

The French Socialist and Communist literature was thus completely emasculated

法国社会主义和共产主义文学就这样被彻底阉割了

in the hands of the German philosophers it ceased to express the struggle of one class with the other

在德国哲学家的手中，它不再表现一个阶级与另一个阶级的斗争

and so the German philosophers felt conscious of having overcome "French one-sidedness"

因此，德国哲学家们意识到已经克服了"法国的片面性"

it did not have to represent true requirements, rather, it represented requirements of truth

它不必代表真实的要求，相反，它代表了真理的要求

there was no interest in the proletariat, rather, there was interest in Human Nature

对无产阶级没有兴趣，相反，对人性感兴趣

the interest was in Man in general, who belongs to no class, and has no reality

兴趣是一般的人，他不属于任何阶级，也没有现实

a man who exists only in the misty realm of philosophical fantasy

一个只存在于哲学幻想的迷雾境界的人

but eventually this schoolboy German Socialism also lost its pedantic innocence

但最终这个小学生德国社会主义也失去了迂腐的纯真

the German Bourgeoisie, and especially the Prussian Bourgeoisie fought against feudal aristocracy

德国资产阶级，特别是普鲁士资产阶级反对封建贵族

the absolute monarchy of Germany and Prussia was also being faught against

德意志和普鲁士的绝对君主制也受到反对

and in turn, the literature of the liberal movement also became more earnest

反过来，自由主义运动的文学也变得更加认真

Germany's long wished-for opportunity for "true" Socialism was offered

德国为"真正的"社会主义提供了人们期待已久的机会

the opportunity of confronting the political movement with the Socialist demands

用社会主义的要求来对抗政治运动的机会

the opportunity of hurling the traditional anathemas against liberalism

向自由主义抛出传统诅咒的机会

the opportunity to attack representative government and Bourgeoisie competition

攻击代议制政府和资产阶级竞争的机会

Bourgeoisie freedom of the press, Bourgeoisie legislation, Bourgeoisie liberty and equality

资产阶级新闻自由，资产阶级立法，资产阶级自由和平等

all of these could now be critiqued in the real world, rather than in fantasy

所有这些现在都可以在现实世界中受到批评，而不是在幻想中

feudal aristocracy and absolute monarchy had long preached to the masses

封建贵族和君主专制长期以来一直向群众宣扬

"the working man has nothing to lose, and he has everything to gain"

"工人没有什么可失去的，他拥有一切可以得到的"

the Bourgeoisie movement also offered a chance to confront these platitudes

资产阶级运动也为面对这些陈词滥调提供了机会

the French criticism presupposed the existence of modern Bourgeoisie society

法国的批评以现代资产阶级社会的存在为前提

Bourgeoisie economic conditions of existence and Bourgeoisie political constitution

资产阶级的经济生存条件和资产阶级政治宪法

the very things whose attainment was the object of the pending struggle in Germany

这些东西的成就正是德国悬而未决的斗争的目标

Germany's silly echo of socialism abandoned these goals just in the nick of time

德国对社会主义的愚蠢回声在时间紧迫的情况下放弃了这些目标

the absolute governments had their following of parsons, professors, country squires and officials

专制政府有他们的追随者帕森斯、教授、乡绅和官员

the government of the time met the German working-class risings with floggings and bullets

当时的政府用鞭笞和子弹来应对德国工人阶级的起义

for them this socialism served as a welcome scarecrow against the threatening Bourgeoisie

对他们来说，这种社会主义是对抗威胁资产阶级的受欢迎的稻草人

and the German government was able to offer a sweet dessert after the bitter pills it handed out

德国政府在分发苦药后能够提供甜食

this "True" Socialism thus served the governments as a weapon for fighting the German Bourgeoisie

因此，这种"真正的"社会主义为政府服务，成为与德国资产阶级作斗争的武器

and, at the same time, it directly represented a reactionary interest; that of the German Philistines

同时，它直接代表了反动的利益;德意志非利士人

In Germany the petty Bourgeoisie class is the real social basis of the existing state of things

在德国，小资产阶级是现存事物的真正社会基础

a relique of the sixteenth century that has constantly been cropping up under various forms

十六世纪的遗迹，不断以各种形式出现

To preserve this class is to preserve the existing state of things in Germany

保持这个阶级就是保持德国的现有状态

The industrial and political supremacy of the Bourgeoisie threatens the petty Bourgeoisie with certain destruction

资产阶级的工业和政治霸权使小资产阶级受到一定的破坏

on the one hand, it threatens to destroy the petty Bourgeoisie

through the concentration of capital
一方面，它威胁要通过资本集中来消灭小资产阶级
on the other hand, the Bourgeoisie threatens to destroy it
through the rise of a revolutionary proletariat
另一方面，资产阶级威胁要通过革命无产阶级的崛起来摧毁它
"True" Socialism appeared to kill these two birds with one
stone. It spread like an epidemic
"真正的"社会主义似乎一石二鸟。它像流行病一样传播
The robe of speculative cobwebs, embroidered with flowers
of rhetoric, steeped in the dew of sickly sentiment
投机的蜘蛛网长袍，绣着修辞的花朵，浸泡在病态情感的露水
中
this transcendental robe in which the German Socialists
wrapped their sorry "eternal truths"
这件超然的长袍，德国社会主义者包裹着他们可悲的"永恒真理
"
all skin and bone, served to wonderfully increase the sale of
their goods amongst such a public
所有的皮肤和骨头，都奇妙地增加了他们的商品在这样的公众
中的销售
And on its part, German Socialism recognised, more and
more, its own calling
就其本身而言，德国社会主义越来越认识到自己的使命
it was called to be the bombastic representative of the petty-
Bourgeoisie Philistine
它被称为小资产阶级非利士人的夸张代表
It proclaimed the German nation to be the model nation, and
German petty Philistine the model man
它宣称德意志民族是模范民族，而德国小非利士人是模范民族
To every villainous meanness of this model man it gave a
hidden, higher, Socialistic interpretation
对于这个模范人物的每一个邪恶的卑鄙行为，它都给出了一种
隐藏的、更高的、社会主义的解释
this higher, Socialistic interpretation was the exact contrary
of its real character
这种更高的社会主义解释与其真实性质完全相反
It went to the extreme length of directly opposing the

"brutally destructive" tendency of Communism

它竭尽全力直接反对共产主义的"残酷破坏性"倾向

and it proclaimed its supreme and impartial contempt of all class struggles

它宣称它对一切阶级斗争的至高无上和公正的蔑视

With very few exceptions, all the so-called Socialist and Communist publications that now (1847) circulate in Germany belong to the domain of this foul and enervating literature

除了极少数例外，现在（1847年）在德国流传的所有所谓的社会主义和共产主义出版物都属于这种肮脏而充满活力的文学作品的范畴

Conservative Socialism, or Bourgeoisie Socialism
保守社会主义，或资产阶级社会主义

A part of the Bourgeoisie is desirous of redressing social grievances
资产阶级的一部分渴望纠正社会不满

in order to secure the continued existence of Bourgeoisie society
为了保证资产阶级社会的继续存在

To this section belong economists, philanthropists, humanitarians
这部分属于经济学家、慈善家、人道主义者

improvers of the condition of the working class and organisers of charity
工人阶级状况的改善者和慈善事业的组织者

members of societies for the prevention of cruelty to animals
防止虐待动物协会成员

temperance fanatics, hole-and-corner reformers of every imaginable kind
节制狂热者，各种可以想象的改革者

This form of Socialism has, moreover, been worked out into complete systems
而且，这种形式的社会主义已经发展成完整的制度

We may cite Proudhon's "Philosophie de la Misère" as an example of this form
我们可以引用蒲鲁东的《悲惨世界哲学》作为这种形式的一个例子

The Socialistic Bourgeoisie want all the advantages of modern social conditions
社会主义资产阶级想要现代社会条件的一切好处

but the Socialistic Bourgeoisie don't necessarily want the resulting struggles and dangers
但社会主义资产阶级并不一定想要由此产生的斗争和危险

They desire the existing state of society, minus its revolutionary and disintegrating elements
他们渴望社会的现有状态，减去其革命和瓦解的因素

in other words, they wish for a Bourgeoisie without a

proletariat
换句话说，他们希望有一个没有无产阶级的资产阶级
The Bourgeoisie naturally conceives the world in which it is supreme to be the best
资产阶级自然而然地设想了一个至高无上的世界，在这个世界里，最好的是至高无上的
and Bourgeoisie Socialism develops this comfortable conception into various more or less complete systems
资产阶级社会主义把这种舒适的概念发展成各种或多或少完整的制度
they would very much like the proletariat to march straightway into the social New Jerusalem
他们非常希望无产阶级直接进入社会的新耶路撒冷
but in reality it requires the proletariat to remain within the bounds of existing society
但实际上，它要求无产阶级保持在现存社会的范围内
they ask the proletariat to cast away all their hateful ideas concerning the Bourgeoisie
他们要求无产阶级抛弃他们对资产阶级的一切仇恨思想
there is a second more practical, but less systematic, form of this Socialism
这种社会主义还有第二种更实际但不那么系统的形式
this form of socialism sought to depreciate every revolutionary movement in the eyes of the working class
这种形式的社会主义试图在工人阶级眼中贬低每一场革命运动
they argue no mere political reform could be of any advantage to them
他们认为，单纯的政治改革对他们没有任何好处
only a change in the material conditions of existence in economic relations are of benefit
只有改变经济关系中的物质生存条件才是有益的
like communism, this form of socialism advocates for a change in the material conditions of existence
与共产主义一样，这种形式的社会主义主张改变物质生存条件
however, this form of socialism by no means suggests the abolition of the Bourgeoisie relations of production
但是，这种形式的社会主义决不是要废除资产阶级的生产关系

the abolition of the Bourgeoisie relations of production can only be achieved through a revolution

资产阶级生产关系的废除只能通过革命来实现

but instead of a revolution, this form of socialism suggests administrative reforms

但是，这种形式的社会主义不是革命，而是行政改革

and these administrative reforms would be based on the continued existence of these relations

这些行政改革将基于这些关系的继续存在

reforms, therefore, that in no respect affect the relations between capital and labour

因此，改革绝不影响资本和劳动的关系

at best, such reforms lessen the cost and simplify the administrative work of Bourgeoisie government

充其量，这种改革只是降低了资产阶级政府的成本，简化了行政工作

Bourgeois Socialism attains adequate expression, when, and only when, it becomes a mere figure of speech

资产阶级社会主义在资产阶级社会主义成为纯粹的修辞手法时，也只有当它成为一种修辞手法时，才能得到充分的表达

Free trade: for the benefit of the working class

自由贸易：为了工人阶级的利益

Protective duties: for the benefit of the working class

保护职责：为了工人阶级的利益

Prison Reform: for the benefit of the working class

监狱改革：为了工人阶级的利益

This is the last word and the only seriously meant word of Bourgeoisie Socialism

这是资产阶级社会主义的最后一句话，也是唯一一句严肃的话

It is summed up in the phrase: the Bourgeoisie is a Bourgeoisie for the benefit of the working class

可以概括为：资产阶级是为工人阶级谋福利的资产阶级

Critical-Utopian Socialism and Communism
批判乌托邦社会主义和共产主义

We do not here refer to that literature which has always
given voice to the demands of the proletariat

我们在这里不是指那种总是表达无产阶级要求的文学

this has been present in every great modern revolution, such
as the writings of Babeuf and others

这在每一次伟大的现代革命中都存在，例如巴贝夫和其他人的
著作

The first direct attempts of the proletariat to attain its own
ends necessarily failed

无产阶级实现自己目的的第一次直接尝试必然失败

these attempts were made in times of universal excitement,
when feudal society was being overthrown

这些尝试是在封建社会被推翻的普遍兴奋时期进行的

the then undeveloped state of the proletariat led to those
attempts failing

当时无产阶级的不发达状态导致了这些尝试的失败

and they failed due to the absence of the economic
conditions for its emancipation

由于缺乏解放的经济条件，他们失败了

conditions that had yet to be produced, and could be
produced by the impending Bourgeoisie epoch alone

这些条件尚未产生，而且可能仅由即将到来的资产阶级时代产
生

The revolutionary literature that accompanied these first
movements of the proletariat had necessarily a reactionary
character

伴随无产阶级的最初运动的革命文学必然具有反动性质

This literature inculcated universal asceticism and social
levelling in its crudest form

这些文学以最粗暴的形式灌输了普遍的禁欲主义和社会平等

The Socialist and Communist systems, properly so called,
spring into existence in the early undeveloped period

社会主义和共产主义制度，恰如其分地称为社会主义和共产主
义制度，是在早期不发达时期出现的

Saint-Simon, Fourier, Owen and others, described the
struggle between proletariat and Bourgeoisie (see Section 1)

圣西门、傅立叶、欧文等人描述了无产阶级和资产阶级之间的
斗争（见第1节）

The founders of these systems see, indeed, the class
antagonisms

这些制度的创始人确实看到了阶级对立

they also see the action of the decomposing elements, in the
prevailing form of society

他们还看到了在社会的普遍形式中分解元素的作用

But the proletariat, as yet in its infancy, offers to them the
spectacle of a class without any historical initiative

但是，无产阶级还处于起步阶段，却向他们展示了一个没有任
何历史主动性的阶级的景象

they see the spectacle of a social class without any
independent political movement

他们看到了一个没有任何独立政治运动的社会阶层的景象

the development of class antagonism keeps even pace with
the development of industry

阶级对立的发展与工业的发展是一致的

so the economic situation does not as yet offer to them the
material conditions for the emancipation of the proletariat

因此，经济形势还没有为他们提供解放无产阶级的物质条件

They therefore search after a new social science, after new
social laws, that are to create these conditions

因此，他们寻找一种新的社会科学，寻找新的社会规律，以创
造这些条件

historical action is to yield to their personal inventive action

历史行动就是屈服于他们个人的创造性行动

historically created conditions of emancipation are to yield
to fantastic conditions

历史上创造的解放条件将屈服于梦幻般的条件

and the gradual, spontaneous class-organisation of the
proletariat is to yield to the organisation of society

无产阶级的渐进的、自发的阶级组织是要屈服于社会组织

the organisation of society specially contrived by these
inventors

这些发明家专门设计的社会组织

Future history resolves itself, in their eyes, into the propaganda and the practical carrying out of their social plans

在他们眼中，未来的历史将自己归结为宣传和实际执行他们的社会计划

In the formation of their plans they are conscious of caring chiefly for the interests of the working class

在制定计划时，他们意识到主要关心工人阶级的利益

Only from the point of view of being the most suffering class does the proletariat exist for them

只有从最受苦阶级的角度来看，无产阶级才为他们而存在

The undeveloped state of the class struggle and their own surroundings inform their opinions

阶级斗争的不发达状态和他们自己的环境影响了他们的意见

Socialists of this kind consider themselves far superior to all class antagonisms

这种社会主义者认为自己远远优于一切阶级对立

They want to improve the condition of every member of society, even that of the most favoured

他们希望改善社会每个成员的状况，甚至是最受宠爱的人的状况

Hence, they habitually appeal to society at large, without distinction of class

因此，他们习惯性地诉诸整个社会，不分阶级

nay, they appeal to society at large by preference to the ruling class

不，他们通过偏爱统治阶级来吸引整个社会

to them, all it requires is for others to understand their system

对他们来说，所需要的只是让其他人了解他们的系统

because how can people fail to see that the best possible plan is for the best possible state of society?

因为人们怎么能看不到最好的计划是为了最好的社会状态呢？

Hence, they reject all political, and especially all revolutionary, action

因此，他们拒绝一切政治行动，特别是一切革命行动

they wish to attain their ends by peaceful means
他们希望通过和平手段达到目的

they endeavour, by small experiments, which are necessarily doomed to failure
他们通过小实验来努力，而这些实验注定要失败

and by the force of example they try to pave the way for the new social Gospel
他们以身作则，试图为新的社会福音铺平道路

Such fantastic pictures of future society, painted at a time when the proletariat is still in a very undeveloped state
在无产阶级还处于非常不发达状态的时候，描绘了未来社会的如此梦幻般的图景

and it still has but a fantastical conception of its own position
它仍然对自己的立场有一个幻想的概念

but their first instinctive yearnings correspond with the yearnings of the proletariat
但是他们最初的本能渴望与无产阶级的渴望是一致的

both yearn for a general reconstruction of society
两人都渴望社会的全面重建

But these Socialist and Communist publications also contain a critical element
但这些社会主义和共产主义出版物也包含一个关键因素

They attack every principle of existing society
他们攻击现存社会的每一个原则

Hence they are full of the most valuable materials for the enlightenment of the working class
因此，它们充满了对工人阶级启蒙的最有价值的材料

they propose abolition of the distinction between town and country, and the family
他们建议废除城乡和家庭的区别

the abolition of the carrying on of industries for the account of private individuals
废除私人经营的工业

and the abolition of the wage system and the proclamation of social harmony
废除工资制度，宣布社会和谐

the conversion of the functions of the State into a mere
superintendence of production
将国家职能转变为纯粹的生产监督

all these proposals, point solely to the disappearance of class
antagonisms
所有这些建议都只指向阶级对立的消失

class antagonisms were, at that time, only just cropping up
当时，阶级对立才刚刚出现

in these publications these class antagonisms are recognised
in their earliest, indistinct and undefined forms only
在这些出版物中，这些阶级对立只是以最早的、模糊的和未定
义的形式被承认

These proposals, therefore, are of a purely Utopian character
因此，这些建议具有纯粹的乌托邦性质

The significance of Critical-Utopian Socialism and
Communism bears an inverse relation to historical
development
批判乌托邦社会主义和共产主义的意义与历史发展呈反比关系

the modern class struggle will develop and continue to take
definite shape
现代阶级斗争将发展并继续形成一定的形式

this fantastic standing from the contest will lose all practical
value
比赛中的这种梦幻般的地位将失去所有实用价值

these fantastic attacks on class antagonisms will lose all
theoretical justification
这些对阶级对立的奇妙攻击将失去所有理论上的正当性

the originators of these systems were, in many respects,
revolutionary
这些系统的鼻祖在许多方面都是革命性的

but their disciples have, in every case, formed mere
reactionary sects
但他们的门徒，在任何情况下，都只是形成了反动的教派

They hold tightly to the original views of their masters
他们紧紧抓住主人的原始观点

but these views are in opposition to the progressive
historical development of the proletariat

但这些观点是同无产阶级的进步历史发展相悖的

They, therefore, endeavour, and that consistently, to deaden the class struggle

因此，他们努力，而且始终如一地扼杀阶级斗争

and they consistently endeavour to reconcile the class antagonisms

他们始终如一地努力调和阶级对立

They still dream of experimental realisation of their social Utopias

他们仍然梦想着通过实验实现他们的社会乌托邦

they still dream of founding isolated "phalansteres" and establishing "Home Colonies"

他们仍然梦想着建立孤立的"方阵"并建立"本土殖民地"

they dream of setting up a "Little Icaria"—duodecimo editions of the New Jerusalem

他们梦想着建立一个"小伊卡里亚"——
新耶路撒冷的十二分之一版本

and they dream to realise all these castles in the air

他们梦想着在空中实现所有这些城堡

they are compelled to appeal to the feelings and purses of the bourgeois

他们不得不迎合资产阶级的感情和钱包

By degrees they sink into the category of the reactionary conservative Socialists depicted above

在某种程度上，他们陷入了上述反动保守社会主义者的范畴

they differ from these only by more systematic pedantry

它们与这些的不同之处仅在于更系统的迂腐

and they differ by their fanatical and superstitious belief in the miraculous effects of their social science

他们的不同之处在于他们对社会科学的神奇效果的狂热和迷信

They, therefore, violently oppose all political action on the part of the working class

因此，他们强烈反对工人阶级的一切政治行动

such action, according to them, can only result from blind unbelief in the new Gospel

根据他们的说法，这种行为只能是盲目地不相信新福音的结果

The Owenites in England, and the Fourierists in France,

respectively, oppose the Chartists and the "Réformistes"
英国的欧文派和法国的傅立叶派分别反对宪章派和"改革派"

Position of the Communists in Relation to the Various Existing

Opposision Parties
共产党人对现有各反对党的立场

Section II has made clear the relations of the Communists to the existing working-class parties
第二节明确了共产党人同现存工人阶级政党的关系

such as the Chartists in England, and the Agrarian Reformers in America
例如英国的宪章派和美国的土地改革派

The Communists fight for the attainment of the immediate aims
共产党人为实现眼前目标而斗争

they fight for the enforcement of the momentary interests of the working class
他们为维护工人阶级的一时利益而斗争

but in the political movement of the present, they also represent and take care of the future of that movement
但在当前的政治运动中，他们也代表并照顾着该运动的未来

In France the Communists ally themselves with the Social-Democrats
在法国，共产党人与社会民主党人结盟

and they position themselves against the conservative and radical Bourgeoisie
他们把自己定位为反对保守和激进的资产阶级

however, they reserve the right to take up a critical position in regard to phrases and illusions traditionally handed down from the great Revolution
但是，他们保留对传统上从大革命中流传下来的短语和幻想采取批评立场的权利

In Switzerland they support the Radicals, without losing sight of the fact that this party consists of antagonistic elements
在瑞士，他们支持激进党，同时又不忽视这个党由敌对分子组成的事实

partly of Democratic Socialists, in the French sense, partly of radical Bourgeoisie

一部分是民主社会主义者，一部分是法国意义上的激进资产阶级

In Poland they support the party that insists on an agrarian revolution as the prime condition for national emancipation

在波兰，他们支持坚持将土地革命作为民族解放的首要条件的政党

that party which fomented the insurrection of Cracow in 1846

1846年煽动克拉科夫起义的政党

In Germany they fight with the Bourgeoisie whenever it acts in a revolutionary way

在德国，只要资产阶级以革命的方式行动，他们就同资产阶级斗争

against the absolute monarchy, the feudal squirearchy, and the petty Bourgeoisie

反对君主专制、封建乡绅和小资产阶级

But they never cease, for a single instant, to instil into the working class one particular idea

但是，他们从未停止过向工人阶级灌输一种特定的思想

the clearest possible recognition of the hostile antagonism between Bourgeoisie and proletariat

尽可能清楚地承认资产阶级和无产阶级之间的敌对对立

so that the German workers may straightaway use the weapons at their disposal

这样德国工人就可以立即使用他们所掌握的武器

the social and political conditions that the Bourgeoisie must necessarily introduce along with its supremacy

资产阶级及其至高无上地位必然引入的社会和政治条件

the fall of the reactionary classes in Germany is inevitable

德国反动阶级的垮台是不可避免的

and then the fight against the Bourgeoisie itself may immediately begin

然后，反对资产阶级本身的斗争可能会立即开始

The Communists turn their attention chiefly to Germany, because that country is on the eve of a Bourgeoisie

revolution
共产党人把注意力主要转向德国，因为德国正处于资产阶级革命的前夜

a revolution that is bound to be carried out under more advanced conditions of European civilisation
一场必然在欧洲文明的更先进条件下进行的革命

and it is bound to be carried out with a much more developed proletariat
它必然要与更发达的无产阶级一起进行

a proletariat more advanced than that of England was in the seventeenth, and of France in the eighteenth century
无产阶级比17世纪的英国和18世纪的法国更先进

and because the Bourgeoisie revolution in Germany will be but the prelude to an immediately following proletarian revolution
因为德国的资产阶级革命只不过是紧随其后的无产阶级革命的前奏

In short, the Communists everywhere support every revolutionary movement against the existing social and political order of things
简言之，各地的共产党人都支持反对现存社会和政治秩序的每一次革命运动

In all these movements they bring to the front, as the leading question in each, the property question
在所有这些运动中，他们把财产问题作为每个运动的主要问题带到了前面

no matter what its degree of development is in that country at the time
无论当时该国的发展程度如何

Finally, they labour everywhere for the union and agreement of the democratic parties of all countries
最后，他们到处为各国民主党派的联合和协议而努力

The Communists disdain to conceal their views and aims
共产党人不屑于隐瞒他们的观点和目标

They openly declare that their ends can be attained only by the forcible overthrow of all existing social conditions
他们公开宣称，只有通过强行推翻所有现存的社会条件，才能

达到他们的目的

Let the ruling classes tremble at a Communistic revolution

让统治阶级在共产主义革命中战战兢兢

The proletarians have nothing to lose but their chains

无产者除了他们的锁链之外，没有什么可失去的

They have a world to win

他们有一个世界可以赢得

WORKING MEN OF ALL COUNTRIES, UNITE!

各国劳动人民，团结起来！

www.ingramcontent.com/pod-product-compliance
Lightning Source LLC
Chambersburg PA
CBHW011743020426
42333CB00024B/3015